The Fishy Prophet

A study of
THE BOOK OF JONAH

By
Rev. Douglas H. Ball, D.Min.

Copyright 2003

INTRODUCTION TO THE BOOK OF JONAH

This began as a personal study. The Lord led me to this book through many avenues, but each converging on this little four-chapter book. It is more than a tale of a man and a large fish. It is more than a struggle of one man and the will of God in his life. It is more than will be shown in all the books written about it. Jonah is about God, His compassion, and His desire that all would love Him and have a personal relationship with Him. It is about being a man of God.

So, let us walk with God in the cool of the evening in the Garden of His Word and, in doing so, learn of Him and know Him better.

Jonah

This little book can be found in the midst of the Minor Prophets, 7 books back from Matthew. In my Bible it is only two whole pages long. A short, sweet story: the kind that men like to read. You can read it in 20 minutes and dwell on it for a life time.

Should we think that this book is of minor consequence because it is stuck in the midst of the Minor Prophets and so short? Not at all. It is not the shortest, nor is it minor. Important things come in small packages.

This short book is the story of a man who is called of God to a specific ministry, gets his back up, and heads the other way. In so doing, he comes face to face with himself, a ship's crew, a large city, and a whale, large fish, or, as Jesus states, sea monster, and is swallowed up, literally and figuratively. After three days he is regurgitated (that's a nice word for "barfed.") onto a beach. He then does what God has called him to do, very reluctantly, leading the great city of Nineveh to a great awakening. At which point, this man becomes angry and pouts. Like most men, Jonah has control issues. Would it not be fantastic for God to send a Jonah today?

Jonah means "Dove." What a name for a man! How's your name? Many men's names have meaning beyond the simplicity of the word. My name, Douglas, means strong or dark depending where you look. Other names such as Joseph (Joe) lean toward Biblical connections. Most men's names are considered names of stature and

JONAH

power either through definition or historical occurrences. But, Dove?????

The dove in Scripture is used to represent Peace or the Holy Spirit, and can carry the idea of meekness, purity, and a splendor of righteousness according to Smith's Bible Dictionary. We can see these ideas in:

Genesis 8

9 But the dove found no rest for the sole of her foot, and she returned unto him into the ark, for the waters were on the face of the whole earth: then he put forth his hand, and took her, and pulled her in unto him into the ark.

10 And he stayed yet other seven days; and again he sent forth the dove out of the ark;

Leviticus 1

14 And if the burnt sacrifice for his offering to the LORD be of fowls, then he shall bring his offering of turtledoves, or of young pigeons.

15 And the priest shall bring it unto the altar, and wring off his head, and burn it on the altar; and the blood thereof shall be wrung out at the side of the altar:

16 And he shall pluck away his crop with his feathers, and cast it beside the altar on the east part, by the place of the ashes:

17 And he shall cleave it with the wings thereof, but shall not divide it asunder: and the priest shall burn it upon the altar, upon the wood that is upon the fire: it is a burnt sacrifice, an offering made by fire, of a sweet savour unto the LORD.

Matthew 3

16 And Jesus, when he was baptized, went up straightway out of the water: and, lo, the heavens were opened unto him, and he saw the Spirit of God descending like a dove, and lighting upon him:

17 And lo a voice from heaven, saying, This is my beloved Son, in whom I am well pleased.

A dove is almost defenseless. The only defense a dove has is God's gift of speed in flight and its ability to change directions very quickly. Due to that speed it burns a lot of calories. Because of its need for all those calories, it spends much time feeding. When it is feeding its eyes are focused on the ground and the dove becomes easy prey for predators. It will also walk obliviously into a trap filled with seeds and become a sacrifice or dinner for some hungry person. A thing to remember if you are ever in a survival situation.

Jonah is very much like a dove in that he is defenseless in himself and only has a chance of survival with God's gifting. You, too, are helpless and vulnerable except for the gifts of God in your life.

Is there the idea that Jonah (Dove) is to bring peace to Israel and/or Nineveh? And/or, is he the defenseless one used of God? These are great questions for us to think on during this discussion.

Nineveh's revival, brought about by God through the ministry of Jonah, did bring Israel another century of peace before Nineveh's fall. Jonah didn't know this when he was called. He didn't know it when he brought about awakening and peace to Nineveh. He didn't even know that when he died.

Do we ever know the complete picture of our ministry as humans when we are called of God?

Do we ever see the total consequences of our following the call of God?

There is a story going around that goes something like this. Some obscure teacher one day led a young man named D. L. Moody to the Lord. Moody in turn led a baseball player named Billy Sunday to that same Lord. Through Sunday's work as an evangelist, a young man named Billy Graham was led to the Lord of Lords. Could a chain like this come from your calling? It did for the obscure teacher who talked with Moody one day, or so the story goes. Just think of the man's astonishment when, in heaven, he learns of the outcome of that simple conversation. What will you possibly be surprised by? Will it be; 1) that you made it? 2) the others there who made it? or, 3) a string of individuals who will be praising God for your part in their salvation?

Every man wants to leave a legacy. What will yours be if your life ended tonight?

Jonah's ministry brought salvation to hundreds of thousands of people. It brought continued peace, even a reprieve from God's judgment, to Israel for almost a hundred years. What a legacy!

Don't you want something like that for your legacy, regardless of whether you know what will happen or not?

This is a trust/faith issue. Do you trust God; have faith in God, enough to answer the call of God in your life with a resounding, YES?

Before we look at this little book, let's find out what do we know about Jonah before this episode in his life.

We know he was a prophet of Israel at the time of Amaziah (796-767 BC).

II Kings 14

23 In the fifteenth year of Amaziah the son of Joash king of Judah Jeroboam the son of Joash king of Israel began to reign in Samaria, and reigned forty and one years.

24 And he did that which was evil in the sight of the LORD: he departed not from all the sins of Jeroboam the son of Nebat, who made Israel to sin.

25 He restored the coast of Israel from the entering of Hamath unto the sea of the plain, according to the word of the LORD God of Israel, which he spake by the hand of his servant Jonah, the son of Amittai, the prophet, which was of Gath-hepher.

26 For the LORD saw the affliction of Israel, that it was very bitter: for there was not any shut up, nor any left, nor any helper for Israel.

27 And the LORD said not that he would blot out the name of Israel from under heaven: but he saved them by the hand of Jeroboam the son of Joash.

The idea that comes to mind at this point is that Jonah may have been just a little fed up with his ministry to the Kings of Israel. They were not being God's men as they should be and Jonah was tired of preaching to sinners that refused to repent. There is also the possibility he even understood that awakening in Nineveh would keep these sinful Kings on the throne of Israel longer, even Isaiah and Jeremiah may have had this same problem at some point in their ministries.

What would your response be if you preached a message over and over again and no one listened or did anything?

Man's wisdom is not God's. God's is better, so much better as to make man's wisdom look like foolishness.

I Corinthians 1

18 For the preaching of the cross is to them that perish foolishness; but unto us which are saved it is the power of God.

19 For it is written, I will destroy the wisdom of the wise, and will bring to nothing the understanding of the prudent.

20 Where is the wise? where is the scribe? where is the disputer of this world? hath not God made foolish the wisdom of this world?

21 For after that in the wisdom of God the world by wisdom knew not God, it pleased God by the foolishness of preaching to save them that believe.

22 For the Jews require a sign, and the Greeks seek after wisdom:

23 But we preach Christ crucified, unto the Jews a stumblingblock, and unto the Greeks foolishness;

24 But unto them which are called, both Jews and Greeks, Christ the power of God, and the wisdom of God.

25 Because the foolishness of God is wiser than men; and the weakness of God is stronger than men.

26 For ye see your calling, brethren, how that not many wise men after the flesh, not many mighty, not many noble, are called:

27 But God hath chosen the foolish things of the world to confound the wise; and God hath chosen the weak things of the world to confound the things which are mighty;

28 And base things of the world, and things which are despised, hath God chosen, yea, and things which are not, to bring to nought things that are:

29 That no flesh should glory in his presence.

We also know that God was going to use him in a mighty way and that he would be an example that Christ would relate to during His first advent.

Luke 11

29 And when the people were gathered thick together, he began to say, This is an evil generation: they seek a sign; and there shall no sign be given it, but the sign of Jonah the prophet.

30 For as Jonah was a sign unto the Ninevites, so shall also the Son of man be to this generation.

It is just too bad the generation Christ spoke to did not respond like Nineveh.

JONAH

Matthew 12

39 But he answered and said unto them, An evil and adulterous generation seeketh after a sign; and there shall no sign be given to it, but the sign of the prophet Jonah:

40 For as Jonah was three days and three nights in the whale's belly; so shall the Son of man be three days and three nights in the heart of the earth.

41 The men of Nineveh shall rise in judgment with this generation, and shall condemn it: because they repented at the preaching of Jonah; and, behold, a greater than Jonah is here.

The believers of Nineveh will judge the Israel of AD 30, just as believers of all ages will judge the angels.

"Generation" calls for a definition. Nineveh had 40 days to repent and then 100 years before being judged. One hundred years would ensure that all that were involved in the revival in Nineveh were dead and gone before the judgment. 100 years could be seen as the life span of a generation from this view point. Israel had 40 years (a Biblical generation) after the death of Christ before their judgment came down on them in AD 70 at the hand of the Roman Legions. Forty years is considered the general duration of a generation from the birth of one until the maturing of the next. Try both definitions when you study the Word and it just might help in your understanding.

The time frame of the story of Jonah is between 800 – 750 BC according to the best sources.

Jonah's ministry has such awesome impact in the Scriptures, Christ will use it as a picture of His ultimate plan of three days in the belly of the earth before His resurrection from the tomb to walk again with His people. Awakening happened to His followers immediately after His resurrection and then spread throughout the world from one person to another. Even the picture of the two disciples looking into the tomb is credited in the Word as the point where John and Peter finally believed.

This little book presents much concerning where we are as God's people. Under Grace each one of us, as believers, are prophets of God. Are we not told to go unto all nations making disciples? That's part of the job of a prophet, to go and tell God's Word. We have God's Word. We are to tell others of it.

Matthew 28

18 And Jesus came and spake unto them, saying, All power is given unto me in heaven and in earth.

19 Go ye therefore, and teach all nations, baptizing them in the name of the Father, and of the Son, and of the Holy Ghost:

20 Teaching them to observe all things whatsoever I have commanded you: and, lo, I am with you alway, even unto the end of the world. Amen.

There are many people all over the world who have not heard God's Word. I know there are people right in my own community, even friends, family and acquaintances, who have never heard. There are folks in your town that have never heard. We get so caught up in the worldly trappings of our faith, Christmas and Easter celebrations with trees, presents and bunnies that we think everyone has to have heard. It just isn't so. To many of our neighbors, Jesus may be just an historical figure like Caesar or Abe Lincoln. To others, He is just a figment of the imagination of those who need a crutch to lean on called religion. To very few, He is alive and working in their lives to allow others the opportunity to meet the Living God. That means you. Are you providing the folks around you with that opportunity with everything about your life? There's a challenge for you.

There are many who call themselves Christians because they were born in America or because Grandma went to church or whatever, but they are lost and don't know it. They don't know the Living Word.

Are we not called to present Christ to them?

Are you heading the other way like Jonah?

The answer to the first question is really "YES." If you will truly examine the second question in the light of the WORD, there is a possibility that the answer to the second question is "YES" also. And, that is the shame of it. How many of us are missing the Joy just as Jonah did?

So, let's get into the book.

The Gospel Call

Jonah 1:1 Now the word of the LORD came unto Jonah the son of Amittai, saying,

2 Arise, go to Nineveh, that great city, and cry against it; for their wickedness is come up before me.

Jonah is called. God hears the cries of the people that Nineveh has been oppressing and calls Jonah to go and give Nineveh His message.

This is not a calling of Jonah to God, but a man's calling to a task for God. The Word tells us that we are saved by Grace through faith and then called to good works for the Kingdom of God.

Ephesians 2

8 For by grace are ye saved through faith; and that not of yourselves: it is the gift of God:

9 Not of works, lest any man should boast.

10 For we are his workmanship, created in Christ Jesus unto good works, which God hath before ordained that we should walk in them.

Right off we can see there are two types of calling. The first is a calling to God, the so called Gospel Call, and the second is a calling for God, the Ministry Call.

Every man has a purpose and a calling before God to a task that God had planned from before the foundations of the earth.

Colossians 1

16 For by him were all things created, that are in heaven, and that are in earth, visible and invisible, whether they be thrones, or dominions, or principalities, or powers: all things were created by him, and for him:

Everything was created by Him, for His purposes, under His dominion. The problem lies in man rejecting God's call in his life. First the Gospel Call is rejected, thereby rejecting any possibility of a Ministry Call. Or, some folks make a big show of a Gospel Call and reject any further calls of God. In which case, is the Gospel Call really being responded to? I think not.

Ecclesiastes 3 tells us when that purpose will be carried out. It will happen in His time.

Ecclesiastes 3

3 To everything there is a season, and a time to every purpose under the heaven:

Many times the Gospel Call comes through loud and clear, and then there is silence for a while. This is a time of growth, a time for reflection, a time for maturing in the Lord. Hang in there, the Ministry Call will come. It may come many times. God doesn't waste His talents on people who hide those talents, instead, He gives many to those who develop them and bear much fruit.

Let's look first at the idea of the Gospel Call.

Romans 10

4 For Christ is the end of the law for righteousness to every one that believeth.

5 For Moses describeth the righteousness which is of the law, That the man which doeth those things shall live by them.

6 But the righteousness which is of faith speaketh on this wise, Say not in thine heart, Who shall ascend into heaven? (that is, to bring Christ down from above:)

7 Or, Who shall descend into the deep? (that is, to bring up Christ again from the dead.)

8 But what saith it? The word is nigh thee, even in thy mouth, and in thy heart: that is, the word of faith, which we preach;

9 That if thou shalt confess with thy mouth the Lord Jesus, and shalt believe in thine heart that God hath raised him from the dead, thou shalt be saved.

10 For with the heart man believeth unto righteousness; and with the mouth confession is made unto salvation.

11 For the scripture saith, Whosoever believeth on him shall not be ashamed.

12 For there is no difference between the Jew and the Greek: for the same Lord over all is rich unto all that call upon him.

13 For whosoever shall call upon the name of the Lord shall be saved.

14 How then shall they call on him in whom they have not believed? and how shall they believe in him of whom they have not heard? and how shall they hear without a preacher?

JONAH

15 And how shall they preach, except they be sent? as it is written, How beautiful are the feet of them that preach the gospel of peace, and bring glad tidings of good things!

16 But they have not all obeyed the gospel. For Esaias saith, Lord, who hath believed our report?

17 So then faith cometh by hearing, and hearing by the word of God.

God is telling us in 4-8 that you don't command God to do things as your servant, but you as His servant have the words you must use to tell the world, in your heart and in your mouth. This is your witness.

Confess Jesus, and believe.

Confess means to agree with the accuser. Satan is the accuser of all sinners. By agreeing with him that you are a sinner, guilty, worthy of death, and then confessing (agreeing that you need a Savior) that Jesus died for your sins and believing that God raised Him from the dead, is the simplicity of the Gospel Call.

It is the same for everyone. Call upon the name of the Lord and thou shalt be saved.

Jonah has heard this call. Have you?

Jonah has responded to that call.

Have you?

Someone was called to preach to you the Gospel Call. You are called to share that same call with others. Don't you want to have beautiful feet (verse 15)?

Ephesians 2

8 For by grace are ye saved through faith; and that not of yourselves: it is the gift of God:

9 Not of works, lest any man should boast.

10 For we are his workmanship, created in Christ Jesus unto good works, which God hath before ordained that we should walk in them.

Salvation is by Grace through faith, plus or minus nothing. You can't work for it. You can't get a job, save all your money and buy it, it is free, Grace through faith, plus or minus nothing.

The Ministry Call

Ephesians 2:10 leads us to the called to good works, the Ministry Call.

Notice that the works comes out of or after salvation, not before or into salvation. A person cannot work their way into the presence of God, into eternity future with Christ, into heaven. People work their way into early graves, into strokes or heart attacks, into hell. No one will ever look back and say, "I should have done more earthly work." Many will look back and say, "I missed/ignored/refused that call. I bore no fruit for the Kingdom of God." They will mourn on judgment day.

Jonah is already called to God. He is working for God and he now gets a call to a new ministry opportunity.

Matthew 5

16 Let your light so shine before men, that they may see your good works, and glorify your Father which is in heaven.

Try personalizing this verse. It helps. It could read, Let my light be seen by men and see my good works and give YOU all the glory, Lord.

2 Timothy 3

17 That the man of God may be perfect, throughly furnished unto all good works.

Hebrews 10

24 And let us consider one another to provoke unto love and to good works:

1 Peter 2

12 Having your conversation honest among the Gentiles: that, whereas they speak against you as evildoers, they may by your good works, which they shall behold, glorify God in the day of visitation.

It is apparent from the above verses that each and every one of us receives at least one Ministry Call.

When God calls there is something that goes with the call.

You might get a Ministry Call and say to yourself, "I just can't do that." When I was seventeen, I was scared to death to talk in front of two or more people, unless they were my buds of course. The time came for me to be on the stage during a high school assembly before the entire student body of 1400 students and faculty. Not only did I forget the words, I forgot completely where I was or why I was there. I was basically led off the stage after a few moments. I can still remember that "deer in the headlights feeling." And, God called me to preach the Word.

God gifts everyone that He calls. And that is exactly what He did for Jonah. He gave Jonah the directions and the abilities to carry out His tasking.

You can ask my congregation. I have never been at a loss for words in the pulpit. They'd most likely tell you they wished God would give me fewer words to share.

As we discuss the Ministry Call, we must look at Gifts.

1 Corinthians 12

4 Now there are diversities of gifts, but the same Spirit.

5 And there are differences of administrations, but the same Lord.

6 And there are diversities of operations, but it is the same God which worketh all in all.

7 But the manifestation of the Spirit is given to every man to profit withal.

Oh, no, this crazy preacher is going to start preaching on the gifts of the Spirit. You can go to the bank with the fact that I am, for one reason and one reason only at this point. I want to say this very clearly and I want you to hear what is said, "God never calls a person that HE doesn't give all the gifts and all the other necessities required to accomplish all HE wants done when HE wants it done." NEVER! HE may not give us the gifts we want or the gifts we think we need, but for what HE needs done, He gives us everything we need to do just that, maybe even more, absolutely positively without a doubt, nothing less.

This passage tells us that all of us are gifted by His Holy Spirit for the benefit of all of us. We have all in all and for all. In other words, He will give all of us gifts that are for the benefit/profit (not financial, but spiritual) of all of us. Stay with me now. My gifts are given to me to profit all of the Body of Christ and your gifts are given to you to profit all of the Body of Christ. When I say Body of Christ, I am including all of the possible members of that Body.

There are many possible gifts the Holy Spirit has in His gift bag to pass out to God's people and He more than generously passes them out, as necessary, to all those to whom they are necessary for the ministry to which they are called. He also gives each believer as many gifts as that person needs to the level or in the quantity that the called person must have to accomplish the work of the Lord for the benefit of all.

So, God makes the decision which gifts we need and in what amount we need them to carry out His work in His time and gives them to the Called through the Power of the Holy Spirit.

As we get back to Jonah, we see that he had already responded to the Gospel Call. He was God's man in Israel. Now, as Jonah hears this Call to Ministry, he knows that God will give him all he needs, when he needs it to get God's job done.

You see, in every congregation there are people being called by the Holy Spirit of God to every different ministry He wants carried out by that congregation. Every one of them is gifted to do that ministry, as God wants it done. Unfortunately, there are many Jonahs in most congregations and they are heading the opposite

JONAH

direction just like Jonah is going to do. In verse 3 of Jonah 1, Jonah not only says, "No!" he packs up and goes the other direction.

Each and every one of us is created by God, for God's glory. Each and every one of us has a task before God. Remember,

Colossians 1

16 For by Him were all things created that are in Heaven or on earth, visible and invisible, whether they be thrones, dominions, or principalities or powers, all things were created by Him and for Him.

All the great catechisms and creeds of Christianity state that man was made for the glory and pleasure of God.

If you are not feeling the pleasure and glory of God in your life, what could be the problem? If you are not feeling God's nearness in your life, who moved? If you feel you are not receiving all the promises of God in your life, take a close look at how you are living the promises you made to God through faith.

Romans 12

1 I beseech you therefore, brethren, by the mercies of God, that ye present your bodies a living sacrifice, holy, acceptable unto God, which is your reasonable service.

2 And be not conformed to this world: but be ye transformed by the renewing of your mind, that ye may prove what is that good, and acceptable, and perfect, will of God.

3 For I say, through the grace given unto me, to every man that is among you, not to think of himself more highly than he ought to

think; but to think soberly, according as God hath dealt to every man the measure of faith.

4 For as we have many members in one body, and all members have not the same office:

5 So we, being many, are one body in Christ, and every one members one of another.

6 Having then gifts differing according to the grace that is given to us, whether prophecy, let us prophesy according to the proportion of faith;

7 Or ministry, let us wait on our ministering: or he that teacheth, on teaching;

8 Or he that exhorteth, on exhortation: he that giveth, let him do it with simplicity; he that ruleth, with diligence; he that sheweth mercy, with cheerfulness.

We are called to sacrifice self as our reasonable, expected service/worship of God. When we call ourselves a Christian, Christ follower/imitator, and we look like the lost who have never known Christ (conformed to the world) we are not proving God's will in our lives or in the Church.

Luke 9

23 And he said to them all, If any man will come after me, let him deny himself, and take up his cross daily, and follow me.

So, when we hear the call of God, we don't present God with an offering and walk in the opposite direction. Instead, we present our lives as a sacrifice to Him.

Galatians 2

20 I am crucified with Christ: nevertheless I live; yet not I, but Christ liveth in me: and the life which I now live in the flesh I live by the faith of the Son of God, who loved me, and gave himself for me.

We express that surrender by doing as He would have us to do when He would have us to do. The problem in many lives, mine for many years, we do like Jonah. We pack our bags, get on a boat, and go in the opposite direction.

I can't help but wonder how many of us are not receiving totally out-of-this-world blessings because we are on a boat, or a bicycle, or a Ford, or a 767, or a pew, going the opposite direction just like Jonah.

We have a serious problem in the church today. We think a church facility is a meeting place for social events that may or may not include some rendering of the Word and nice platitudes or lifestyle judgments for other folks.

The Church, the Body of Christ, is a training ground for servants and ministers. When we attend a meeting, we should be getting trained to Go, make disciples, teaching, and baptizing. We are not there to get our ears tickled or to get our weekly warm fuzzy.

1 Peter 4

10 As every man hath received the gift, even so minister the same one to another, as good stewards of the manifold grace of God.

11 *If any man speak, let him speak as the oracles of God; if any man minister, let him do it as of the ability which God giveth: that God in all things may be glorified through Jesus Christ, to whom be praise and dominion for ever and ever. Amen.*

Peter talks here that you have received the gift of God in your life. First you received the gift of salvation by God's Grace through faith, plus or minus nothing. Then you receive a calling and the gifts to do the ministry to which you have been called. Now that you have gotten those gifts, what are you going to do with them? Many just continue to sit in the pew.

He tells us to minister to each other with them, being good stewards of all God has given us. We are to do this to the best of the ability that God has given us to His glory.

What does it mean to minister? It doesn't mean to stand behind the pulpit and present a sermon. It doesn't mean to wear a funny collar or robe. (Although, both of those might be a part of your calling.) Minister means to serve.

Many churches have a motto or statement on their bulletins or in their constitution and bylaws that goes something like this, "Every member a minister." What they are saying is that we are all called to service of some kind. God calls us to servanthood, not to pride, not to personal glory, but to servanthood. We serve Him by serving others in His name to His glory.

We are to do this as good stewards of the complete Grace of God. Stewards are ones who care for the property of the master or owner of that property in His stead. The gifts that you have received are the property of someone else. You are the property of someone else. God is the owner of you and all you are and all you possess. You are the steward of you and all that you are and all you possess. You have been bought with a price. God wants you to use you and all that you are and all you possess to His glory by serving Him.

1 Corinthians 6

20 For ye are bought with a price: therefore glorify God in your body, and in your spirit, which are God's.

1 Corinthians 7

23 Ye are bought with a price; be not ye the servants of men.

1 Peter 4 tells us to speak for the Lord, speak the Lord's words. If we are called to serve, to serve with all the ability we are given. What do you have that God has given you to serve with? Perhaps a car, a house, health, strength, special gifts and talents; but are you using it to the best of the ability that God has given you?

Have you heard and responded to the Gospel Call?

If you have, have you heard the Ministry Call? Many have, but many have not. God is calling *all* of His people to some ministry. I do not believe there is a ministry of sitting in the pews, or staying home on Sundays, or being your own congregation, unless you are the only Christian for many miles around and then it is your ministry to build a group through your witness.

What has been your response to the Ministry Call and gifting?

What are you going to do now?

Will that glorify God?

If not, pray again.

Jonah's Call

Jonah 1:1 Now the word of the LORD came unto Jonah the son of Amittai, saying,

2 Arise, go to Nineveh, that great city, and cry against it; for their wickedness is come up before me.

Let's look at Nineveh and their wickedness for a moment.

Nimrod established Nineveh. You remember Nimrod don't you? When I was in the service, a Nimrod was one who wasn't very bright. Seems to fit here.

Genesis 10

8 And Cush (second from Noah in the line of Ham and remember that Ham was the cursed son) **begat Nimrod: he began to be a mighty one in the earth.**

9 He was a mighty hunter before the LORD: wherefore it is said, Even as Nimrod the mighty hunter before the LORD.

10 And the beginning of his kingdom was Babel, and Erech, and Accad, and Calneh, in the land of Shinar.

11 Out of that land went forth Asshur (went forth out of Assyria), and builded Nineveh, and the city Rehoboth, and Calah,

12 And Resen between Nineveh and Calah: the same is a great city.

JONAH

The context of this last verse gives us three cities in one, a great metropolitan area. This is what Jonah was to enter.

Nimrod is the same man who caused the difficulty in Babel.

The people began to look upon him as being more important than the creator God they knew from Noah's testimony. He accepted that position. Satan had the same problem.

Genesis 11

1 And the whole earth was of one language, and of one speech.

2 And it came to pass, as they journeyed from the east, that they found a plain in the land of Shinar; and they dwelt there.

3 And they said one to another, Go to, let us make brick, and burn them throughly. And they had brick for stone, and slime had they for morter.

4 And they said, Go to, let us build us a city and a tower, whose top may reach unto heaven; and let us make us a name, lest we be scattered abroad upon the face of the whole earth.

5 And the LORD came down to see the city and the tower, which the children of men builded.

6 And the LORD said, Behold, the people is one, and they have all one language; and this they begin to do: and now nothing will be restrained from them, which they have imagined to do.

7 Go to, let us go down, and there confound their language, that they may not understand one another's speech.

8 So the LORD scattered them abroad from thence upon the face of all the earth: and they left off to build the city.

9 Therefore is the name of it called Babel; because the LORD did there confound the language of all the earth: and from thence did the LORD scatter them abroad upon the face of all the earth.

Notice that Genesis 10:10 says that the beginning of his kingdom was Babel . . .

Nimrod is also of the line of Ham, Noah's son. This line could be called the "Cursed Line." Let's look at Ham.

Genesis 9

20 And Noah began to be an husbandman, and he planted a vineyard:

21 And he drank of the wine, and was drunken; and he was uncovered within his tent.

22 And Ham, the father of Canaan, saw the nakedness of his father, and told his two brethren without.

23 And Shem and Japheth took a garment, and laid it upon both their shoulders, and went backward, and covered the nakedness of their father; and their faces were backward, and they saw not their father's nakedness.

24 And Noah awoke from his wine, and knew what his younger son had done unto him.

25 And he said, Cursed be Canaan; a servant of servants shall he be unto his brethren.

26 And he said, Blessed be the LORD God of Shem; and Canaan shall be his servant.

27 God shall enlarge Japheth, and he shall dwell in the tents of Shem; and Canaan shall be his servant.

JONAH

There is a parallel here between Ham and Ishmael. These two are children of devout men.

Ishmael is the son of Abraham, through Hagar, when Abraham and Sarah took matters into their own hands because they were tired of waiting for God to produce the promised son, Isaac, (Genesis 16). War has existed between the descendants of Ishmael, the child of man's doing, and the children of Isaac, the child of promise from God ever since. This war ravages the Middle East even today between Israel and the surrounding nations.

Ishmael may be seen as the world and its ideas while Isaac represents the Kingdom of God and its glory. Not that the individuals are evil or Godly, but that the paths of their lives represent those things. In God's way is blessing, while in man's way is curse.

In Ham we see that he is the middle son of Noah, but has worldly ideas on how to get things done. The first son, Shem, is the line of the King of Kings. The worldly line, Ham, and the blessed line, Shem, have been at war ever since as the ideas of the world make war against the King of Kings and the Kingdom of God. Canaan was the son of Ham and God sent Israel out of Egypt to bring judgment on Canaan.

So, Nimrod is the founder of Nineveh. Nimrod is the grandson of Ham. Nimrod is a problem. Nineveh will be used of God one day to bring judgment on Israel. But, God has something against Nineveh at this time.

The book of Nahum is written against Nineveh. Parts of Micah also concern this city.

Nahum 3

1 Woe to the bloody city! it is all full of lies and robbery; the prey departeth not;

2 The noise of a whip, and the noise of the rattling of the wheels, and of the pransing horses, and of the jumping chariots.

3 The horseman lifteth up both the bright sword and the glittering spear: and there is a multitude of slain, and a great number of carcases; and there is none end of their corpses; they stumble upon their corpses:

4 Because of the multitude of the whoredoms of the wellfavoured harlot, the mistress of witchcrafts, that selleth nations through her whoredoms, and families through her witchcrafts.

5 Behold, I am against thee, saith the LORD of hosts; and I will discover thy skirts upon thy face, and I will shew the nations thy nakedness, and the kingdoms thy shame.

6 And I will cast abominable filth upon thee, and make thee vile, and will set thee as a gazingstock.

7 And it shall come to pass, that all they that look upon thee shall flee from thee, and say, Nineveh is laid waste: who will bemoan her? whence shall I seek comforters for thee?

8 Art thou better than populous No, that was situate among the rivers, that had the waters round about it, whose rampart was the sea, and her wall was from the sea?

9 Ethiopia and Egypt were her strength, and it was infinite; Put and Lubim were thy helpers.

10 Yet was she carried away, she went into captivity: her young children also were dashed in pieces at the top of all the streets: and

JONAH

they cast lots for her honourable men, and all her great men were bound in chains.

Micah 5

2 But thou, Bethlehem Ephratah, though thou be little among the thousands of Judah, yet out of thee shall he come forth unto me that is to be ruler in Israel; whose goings forth have been from of old, from everlasting.

3 Therefore will he give them up, until the time that she which travaileth hath brought forth: then the remnant of his brethren shall return unto the children of Israel.

4 And he shall stand and feed in the strength of the LORD, in the majesty of the name of the LORD his God; and they shall abide: for now shall he be great unto the ends of the earth.

5 And this man shall be the peace, when the Assyrian shall come into our land: and when he shall tread in our palaces, then shall we raise against him seven shepherds, and eight principal men.

6 And they shall waste the land of Assyria with the sword, and the land of Nimrod in the entrances thereof: thus shall he deliver us from the Assyrian, when he cometh into our land, and when he treadeth within our borders.

Nineveh was the capital of the Assyrian empire located on the Tigris River in what is now Mosul, Iraq. It was the world power of the time. The ruins of Nineveh are at the outskirts of today's Mosul in modern Iraq.

Nineveh was extremely cruel. Victims within the city walls of a town that Assyria attacked would commit suicide rather than be captured. When Nineveh did capture a community, those that survived the battle were subject to various levels of torture. All males were killed or mutilated. Children were burned alive. Women were kept as long as they were healthy. Kings of conquered territories were taken back to the capital and flayed alive before the king's court.

The King, Assur-nasir-pal II, before Jonah was born, said, "In strife and conflict I besieged and conquered the city. I felled 3,000 of their fighting men with the sword. I carried off prisoners, possessions, oxen and cattle from them. I burnt many captives from them. I captured many troops alive: I cut off some of their arms and hands, I cut off of others their noses and ears. I gouged out the eyes of many troops. I made one pile of living and one of heads. I hung their heads on trees around the city. I burnt their adolescent boys and girls." Sounds like a real nice guy.

Telling Jonah to go witness to them is like asking a holocaust Jew to go witness to the Nazis in 1945.

These were just the people we would all love to witness to, just like the Jihadists in the world today.

At this point in time, Nineveh's armies had been making attacks into the Northern Kingdom of Israel. (I can't help but wonder, had Jonah's family been brutalized by these people?) (Love one another. Love your enemies. These commands of Jesus come to mind here.)

Jonah had no love for Nineveh, none whatsoever.

JONAH

Nineveh had crossed God's line. He wasn't letting them continue. He was calling Jonah to go and give Nineveh His message.

Jonah's only motivation was that he wanted to see them destroyed by God's judgment.

God's call is experienced in many ways, but five things are common to all calls seen in the Word:

God's method is unique to each one called.

It was known to be God's call when it happened.

The one hearing knew what God was saying.

The one called knew exactly what was required.

A fifth thing is found out very quickly. God gifts those called with all they need to get His job done in His time.

It appears that Jonah may have been sleeping when he received this call. He is told to rise up. Perhaps he was just reclining or resting.

Others have received their calls through various methods. Check these out.

> Dreams – Genesis 28:10-15
> A loud voice – 1 Samuel 3
> Angels – Genesis 16, Luke 2:8-15
> A whisper – 1 Kings 19:12

With each of these methods, and more, God presents His call and the five traits listed above are always there.

When we look at those five traits of God's calling and the methods from Scripture, we see that there is no set method of call, but the traits will be there. This makes the idea of wondering what God's call is for one's life a bit more definite than most folks want to accept.

I have heard many people wondering if this was God's call, or if that was God's call. This or That, This or That.

The only surety we have is that the method of call varies, we will know He is calling, we will understand what is said and we will know exactly what we are to do. Through faith we also know that because it is God's call for us, we will receive all the gifts that are necessary to do the task God's way in God's time. It may not be our idea of what is required to get the job done, but it is God's.

At that point the choice is ours.

We are all called to some ministry. You know it when it happens. You know exactly what God is saying. You know exactly what you are to do. You have the faith to know that God will give you all the gifts you need to do His job in His time.

What are you going to do?

Jonah's Response

Jonah 1:3 But Jonah rose up to flee unto Tarshish from the presence of the LORD, and went down to Joppa; and he found a ship going to Tarshish: so he paid the fare thereof, and went down into it, to go with them unto Tarshish from the presence of the LORD.

Jonah obeys the part about rising up and then goes the other direction. Partial obedience is disobedience.

Tarshish was in Southern Spain or, as some believe, in Greece. In either case, Tarshish is west and Nineveh is east from Israel. Some writings equate Tarshish with Carthage, but this is disputed by most.

Was this a safe place for Jonah?

Where is your safe place?

Do you retreat there to get away from God or to be with God?

Can we hide from God?

So, where is the presence of God?

Psalm 139

7 Whither shall I go from thy spirit? or whither shall I flee from thy presence?

8 If I ascend up into heaven, thou art there: if I make my bed in hell, behold, thou art there.

9 If I take the wings of the morning, and dwell in the uttermost parts of the sea;

10 Even there shall thy hand lead me, and thy right hand shall hold me.

11 If I say, Surely the darkness shall cover me; even the night shall be light about me.

12 Yea, the darkness hideth not from thee; but the night shineth as the day: the darkness and the light are both alike to thee.

Since the darkness cannot hide from God, nothing or no one can hide from God. Many have tried to hide from Almighty God and none have ever succeeded. There is no place or time or attitude or any other idea which will allow you to hide from God. The day will come when God will make His presence known to you and you will be required to make a choice, surrender or continue in spiritual death.

Romans 1

18 For the wrath of God is revealed from heaven against all ungodliness and unrighteousness of men, who hold the truth in unrighteousness.

JONAH

19 Because that which may be known of God is manifest in them; for God hath shewed it unto them.

20 For the invisible things of him from the creation of the world are clearly seen, being understood by the things that are made, even his eternal power and Godhead; so that they are without excuse:

Did the ease of finding space on a boat and having the funds tell Jonah that this was the will of God that he go to Tarshish?

Jeremiah 17

9 The heart is deceitful above all things, and desperately wicked: who can know it?

Can this choice of Jonah's be the Lord's will?

Many Christians today believe the idea that you just keep moving looking for open doors and closed doors to determine the Lord's will. The ship's passage Jonah needed to get him to Tarshish, a couple thousand miles in the wrong direction, only happened once or twice a year due to the weather patterns of the Mediterranean Ocean. But, here's Jonah, walks right up and buys a ticket, no problem.

Open door? No way! Jonah opened this door all on his own. It goes with the idea when we say, "Okay, God, this is what I want to do, bless me." And then, we take steps on our own. On our own is called Godlessness. Godlessness is sin.

God's will? No way!

Many need to reevaluate the ideas on open and closed doors. Search the Word and examine this issue in its light. There you will find that Satan can provide open doors only too well. Should we walk through those? No!

Let's take two examples. The first is that I love to go shooting with a couple of friends now and then. There I am with a loaded gun in my hand and the opportunity to shoot someone. Is that what God would have me to do? I really don't think so because His Word says, "Thou shall not kill." The second is the Tree of the Knowledge of Good and Evil. God left the opportunity to eat of that tree open. There was no fence around it. It was there in the midst of the Garden for all to see.

Did He mean it when He said do not eat of that tree?

Why did He leave the door open?

Is that the test we are to use?

Jonah paid the fare, not God. God pays the fare on journeys for Him. God does provide all that we have, but how we use it is up to us. Here we run into being good stewards of the Grace of God.

George Barna's studies have shown that the average church going family gives less than $300 per year back to the Lord. That's about 1% of income which makes for mighty skimpy pickings for the Lord. He asks for the first fruits. He asks for a tithe, one tenth. He asks for free will offerings from our heart, not the lint from our pockets.

Jonah set his course away from God.

1 Samuel 10:17-27 discusses Saul's inauguration. He hid.

Did Jonah fear failure? Saul did.

There are three reasons for failure to surrender to the will of God in your life:

Pride

Fear

Confusion

Faith delivers us from all three of these.

The problem is surrender. None of us want to surrender or submit to anything. Think of the clamber in the news media when the Southern Baptist Convention adopted a resolution from Ephesians 5, which included "Wives submit yourselves . . ." The view of our day is that surrender and submission, along with obedience, carry the connotation of loser, wimp, and/or lack of success.

Even Jonah had a problem with surrender and he had been serving God for quite a while. The surest symptoms of surrender to the will of God are, "Trust and obey, for there's no other way . . ."

Do you fear failure?

Saul did. Moses appears to have feared not being able to do the job. David constantly cried out for help. James discusses wisdom, as does Solomon in Proverbs.

Why do you fear failure when we have these promises?

Philippians 4

13 I can do all things through Christ which strengtheneth me.

Some folks translate this as – *Everything I do I do through Christ who is my strength.* Does that sound the way you feel about your works?

John 15

4 Abide in me, and I in you. As the branch cannot bear fruit of itself, except it abide in the vine; no more can ye, except ye abide in me.

2 Corinthians 3

4 And such trust have we through Christ to God-ward:

5 Not that we are sufficient of ourselves to think any thing as of ourselves; but our sufficiency is of God;

Our righteousness is as filthy rags. Our strength is nothing. Our thinking is stinking. Our words are without value. We do nothing right of ourselves. All righteousness is of God. Compared to God we are so puny.

Even as Christians, our works, done of ourselves, are stubble. They will be burned at the Judgment Seat of Christ.

2 Corinthians 3

6 Who also hath made us able ministers of the new testament; not of the letter, but of the spirit: for the letter killeth, but the spirit giveth life.

Hebrews 4

16 Let us therefore come boldly unto the throne of grace, that we may obtain mercy, and find grace to help in time of need.

In this case, grace is to say, "all sufficiency." Why go without when you can have it all, in Christ? God's all is never the same as man's all.

JONAH

Isaiah 41

10 Fear thou not; for I am with thee: be not dismayed; for I am thy God: I will strengthen thee; yea, I will help thee; yea, I will uphold thee with the right hand of my righteousness.

Jesus promised, *"I will never leave thee..."*

Jesus' Great Commission says, *"I am with you to the end of the age."*

Without Him where are we? We are lost.

Jonah had certainly lost his direction.

John 1

3 All things were made by him; and without him was not any thing made that was made.

Colossians 1

16 For by him were all things created, that are in heaven, and that are in earth, visible and invisible, whether they be thrones, or dominions, or principalities, or powers: all things were created by him, and for him:

17 And he is before all things, and by him all things consist.

The Maker knows every nook and cranny of His creation. He is even holding it all together.

So, what can we do?

John 5

19 Then answered Jesus and said unto them, Verily, verily, I say unto you, The Son can do nothing of himself, but what he seeth the Father do: for what things soever he doeth, these also doeth the Son likewise.*

John 15

5 I am the vine, ye are the branches: He that abideth in me, and I in him, the same bringeth forth much fruit: for without me ye can do nothing.

His way must be our way and that is the only way we do anything of value. Jonah ran from the presence of the Lord.

Is he out of God's will (backslider), or in total denial of God and His Grace?

Haven't we all gone in the opposite direction at one time or another, or even many times?

Isaiah 53

6 All we like sheep have gone astray; we have turned every one to his own way; and the LORD hath laid on him the iniquity of us all.

Therefore, even Jonah's sins were laid on Christ.

So, why did Jonah run the other way?

Jonah 4:2 And he prayed unto the LORD, and said, I pray thee, O LORD, was not this my saying, when I was yet in my country? Therefore I fled before unto Tarshish: for I knew that thou art a gracious God, and merciful, slow to anger, and of great kindness, and repentest thee of the evil.

JONAH

The message of the book of Jonah is God's great compassion. Jonah went the other way because he knew that if Nineveh repented God would not destroy them.

Is that why we don't witness to our neighbors? Our friends? Our loved ones? Are we afraid they will repent and God will forgive them? After all, they have been our measuring stick for a long time. You know what I mean. We look at them and say to ourselves, "I'm better than they are, so I'm okay," or something similar.

Is that why we ignore or say "no" to God's call in our life? Is the problem that those folks in lower Slobovia, to which we are called as witnesses, might repent and be saved. Why, heavens to mergatroids, we may have to even spend eternity with them folks!

Look a Mary's response to her call.

Luke 1

26 And in the sixth month the angel Gabriel was sent from God unto a city of Galilee, named Nazareth,

27 To a virgin espoused to a man whose name was Joseph, of the house of David; and the virgin's name was Mary.

28 And the angel came in unto her, and said, Hail, thou that art highly favoured, the Lord is with thee: blessed art thou among women.

29 And when she saw him, she was troubled at his saying, and cast in her mind what manner of salutation this should be.

30 And the angel said unto her, Fear not, Mary: for thou hast found favour with God.

31 And, behold, thou shalt conceive in thy womb, and bring forth a son, and shalt call his name JESUS.

32 He shall be great, and shall be called the Son of the Highest: and the Lord God shall give unto him the throne of his father David:

33 And he shall reign over the house of Jacob for ever; and of his kingdom there shall be no end.

34 Then said Mary unto the angel, How shall this be, seeing I know not a man?

35 And the angel answered and said unto her, The Holy Ghost shall come upon thee, and the power of the Highest shall overshadow thee: therefore also that holy thing which shall be born of thee shall be called the Son of God.

36 And, behold, thy cousin Elisabeth, she hath also conceived a son in her old age: and this is the sixth month with her, who was called barren.

37 For with God nothing shall be impossible.

38 And Mary said, Behold the handmaid of the Lord; be it unto me according to thy word. And the angel departed from her.

Jonah didn't respond, "be it unto me . . ." but Mary did. Many will and have walked in the Joy of the Lord because of that response.

Look at Isaiah's response.

Isaiah 6

6 Then flew one of the seraphims unto me, having a live coal in his hand, which he had taken with the tongs from off the altar:

7 And he laid it upon my mouth, and said, Lo, this hath touched thy lips; and thine iniquity is taken away, and thy sin purged.

8 Also I heard the voice of the Lord, saying, Whom shall I send, and who will go for us? Then said I, Here am I; send me.

Here am I send me. Simple isn't it. So, why do so many of us go the other way when God calls? It's almost as if God has bad breath or something.

Attention Getter

Jonah 1:4 But the LORD sent out a great wind into the sea, and there was a mighty tempest in the sea, so that the ship was like to be broken.

God knew exactly where Jonah was. That's where He sent the attention getter (wind) and discipline.

Luke 12

2 For there is nothing covered, that shall not be revealed; neither hid, that shall not be known.

3 Therefore whatsoever ye have spoken in darkness shall be heard in the light; and that which ye have spoken in the ear in closets shall be proclaimed upon the housetops.

This is one of the scarier passages of Scripture. Nothing will remain hidden. All will be revealed. All the secrets we think we have will be right out in the open in living color, for all to see. And, all the time we think that we have gotten away with it, whatever it is. God knows.

There is a blessing in all of this. When this happens, we will no longer bear the burden of keeping all of this in our minds, we will no longer have to work so hard to keep it hidden. A load of pain and a burden of suffering will be lifted. This is why God's forgiveness is so totally wonderful. All our burdens are gone. His load is light, remember. (Matthew 11:28-30)

1 Corinthians 4

5 Therefore judge nothing before the time, until the Lord come, who both will bring to light the hidden things of darkness, and will make manifest the counsels of the hearts: and then shall every man have praise of God.

Even the secret thoughts of our minds will be purged and we will have total praise for God. No longer will we carry the burden of that sin, that secret, and finally we are freed to truly praise God in all things as His child should.

This isn't the only time God has used a storm at sea to make a point. God raised up a couple of other storms for His glory.

Matthew 14

25 And in the fourth watch of the night Jesus went unto them, walking on the sea.

26 And when the disciples saw him walking on the sea, they were troubled, saying, It is a spirit; and they cried out for fear.

27 But straightway Jesus spake unto them, saying, Be of good cheer; it is I; be not afraid.

28 And Peter answered him and said, Lord, if it be thou, bid me come unto thee on the water.

29 And he said, Come. And when Peter was come down out of the ship, he walked on the water, to go to Jesus.

30 But when he saw the wind boisterous, he was afraid; and beginning to sink, he cried, saying, Lord, save me.

31 And immediately Jesus stretched forth his hand, and caught him, and said unto him, O thou of little faith, wherefore didst thou doubt?

32 And when they were come into the ship, the wind ceased.

If by chance you should want a great commentary on this passage, I recommend John Ortberg's, "IF YOU WANT TO WALK ON WATER, YOU GOTTA GET OUT OF THE BOAT."

Look at the lessons in this storm at sea.

Mark 4

36 And when they had sent away the multitude, they took him even as he was in the ship. And there were also with him other little ships.

37 And there arose a great storm of wind, and the waves beat into the ship, so that it was now full.

38 And he was in the hinder part of the ship, asleep on a pillow: and they awake him, and say unto him, Master, carest thou not that we perish?

39 And he arose, and rebuked the wind, and said unto the sea, Peace, be still. And the wind ceased, and there was a great calm.

40 And he said unto them, Why are ye so fearful? how is it that ye have no faith?

41 And they feared exceedingly, and said one to another, What manner of man is this, that even the wind and the sea obey him?

Please notice that the disciples never answer Jesus' question about faith. Why is it we don't want to search our hearts and answer the real questions of life? We would rather ponder the supernatural than examine our natural hearts. Remember, the Bible says that if we would examine ourselves, we would not have to be judged (1 Corinthians 11:31). We are generally more than willing to examine everything and everybody except ourselves. God really asks a lot, doesn't He.

God has the power over all of His creation.

Mark 4

39 And he arose, and rebuked the wind, and said unto the sea, Peace, be still. And the wind ceased, and there was a great calm.

Exodus 14

15 And the LORD said unto Moses, Wherefore criest thou unto me? speak unto the children of Israel, that they go forward:

16 But lift thou up thy rod, and stretch out thine hand over the sea, and divide it: and the children of Israel shall go on dry ground through the midst of the sea.

Psalm 29:

9 The voice of the LORD maketh the hinds to calve, and discovereth the forests: and in his temple doth every one speak of his glory.

10 The LORD sitteth upon the flood; yea, the LORD sitteth King for ever.

Psalm 93

4 The LORD on high is mightier than the noise of many waters, yea, than the mighty waves of the sea.

Proverbs 8

29 When he gave to the sea his decree, that the waters should not pass his commandment: when he appointed the foundations of the earth:

Psalm 89

9 Thou rulest the raging of the sea: when the waves thereof arise, thou stillest them.

Nahum 1

4 He rebuketh the sea, and maketh it dry, and drieth up all the rivers: Bashan languisheth, and Carmel, and the flower of Lebanon languisheth.

5 The mountains quake at him, and the hills melt, and the earth is burned at his presence, yea, the world, and all that dwell therein.

JONAH

Luke 17

1 Then said he unto the disciples, It is impossible but that offences will come: but woe unto him, through whom they come!

2 It were better for him that a millstone were hanged about his neck, and he cast into the sea, than that he should offend one of these little ones.

Jonah's choice is now affecting others. Jonah's sin affects all those around him. Your sin affects many others.

I have heard folks discuss sins they seriously believed did not bother anyone else. Sometimes pornography is listed as a victimless sin. Or, the thoughts of the mind are thought of as not involving anyone else.

But, Christ said that the words of your mouth come from the mind (heart). So, as you think, so you speak. If your thoughts are evil then your words and deeds will be also. That brings others into the picture very quickly. Or, what about the wife of the man involved in porn? She suffers from his demands or lack of attention to her. The continual viewing of porn has been linked to sex crimes against children and women.

There are no victimless crimes/sins. No matter how you rationalize it, at the very least you are the victim of your own hidden secrets.

God will not allow you or Jonah to continue in sin without a serious attempt at bringing you back on track. Hebrews 12:5-8 applies to this idea. God brings us trials to grow our faith and allows us trials to bring us back on track with Him. That is why we are told in James 1:3 to count it all joy when we suffer many trials.

The Mediterranean is a very rough sea. It is shallow with winds coming from all directions and all climates. One wind comes down off the ice cold Alps, cold and wet, and another comes ripping across the Sahara, hot and dry. They meet in the middle. The sea is torn from two or more directions at the same time frequently. Even well-made modern ships are torn apart by a natural storm on this sea.

God sent this storm. This is an attention getter. This storm is supernatural and the crew of this small boat knows that, but don't know why.

How many times have you been caught in the storms of life and not known why?

Could there be someone on the same boat that is out of the will of God?

Could it be you?

When God sends an attention getter, it is supernatural, something that cannot be explained in the normal realm of things. This is a God thing and when God speaks through His attention getters, we had better listen, whether we are the focus or not.

Who's Attention??

Jonah 1:5 Then the mariners were afraid, and cried every man unto his god, and cast forth the wares that were in the ship into the sea, to lighten it of them. But Jonah was gone down into the sides of the ship; and he lay, and was fast asleep.

So, whose attention is God getting with this storm? Jonah is the obvious answer, but don't you think He is catching the attention of the sailors on the ship, also?

The sailors didn't know God as the creator of the universe. They didn't know Him at any level except from the waterfront conversations they have had. Or, did they have a seriously distorted view of God because of their lack of knowledge. In any case, God is pursuing the sailors as well as Jonah.

These sailors feared death and each had his own god and none of their gods could do anything with this sea. It stormed on in spite of their prayers. And, you can believe these men were lifting up prayers before their gods with all their ability. It was that kind of a day.

The sailors knew this was not a natural storm. They knew it was a supernatural one.

Here we see man's ideas for saving himself. Lighten the ship. Their own efforts may only save themselves physically.

When we look into the spiritual realm in trying to save ourselves, we find book after book on the self-help shelves of the bookstore, which promise that if you will only do what they are telling you, you will be all right. Just look around and you will see the pseudo-psycho-babble of do-it-yourself spirituality and designer gods being peddled like the patent medicines of a few decades back.

We find ourselves doing two things in order to lighten the ship of our life in order to bring ourselves into spirituality and save ourselves.

We figure if we're good enough we will make out all right. We do all kinds of great things that bring praise, plaques and medals from our peers. We look inward for the power to be somebody and work within the realm and limitations of this present life.

We figure that if we just get rid of the things that offend God, we can meet Him at the judgment seat and He will greet us with open arms.

How many of our neighbors think they can work their way upward? They say to themselves, "If I go work in the soup kitchen, God will be pleased," or something similar. Paul says in 1 Corinthians 13 that even if he gave all he had to the poor and his body to be burned and had not love, all is wasted effort. Because God is love, without God, nothing avails for salvation. You can't even love enough to meet God.

JONAH

Little do these people know that they can do all kinds of great works and if they are not in the will of God, they are worthless. Jonah could be going to Tarshish to preach the Word of God before millions and still be out of the will of God. This is Jonah's problem, he is out of the will of God. Could this be your problem? Maybe, it is the problem of your neighbor.

So, how much is good enough, anyhow? Read Andy Stanley's book, HOW GOOD IS GOOD ENOUGH.

How many say, "When I quit _____, I'll talk about God or come to church or get saved. I'll be good enough for God then."

HA!

Perhaps Jonah thinks he is too fat for God to use in Nineveh. So he is going to Tarshish to the spa and get in shape for this vigorous ministry. After all, walking 60 miles and preaching all the way is hard work. Even with the best of excuses, he is still out of the will of God.

Many sleep through the call of God to them. They sit in the pew and catch a nap, or they stay at home in bed instead of going to Church at all. Maybe they even turn a blind eye and a deaf ear to the sincere witness of a loved one or friend. Jonah turned a deaf ear to God and went to sleep.

The sailors are locked into totally set procedures; worldly procedures, manmade procedures of salvation from the storms of life. The New Age movement has a bunch of these. These are also one of the top signs of a cult. Rituals to get God's favor, watch out for them.

The plan of action for them is that if a big storm comes up you throw everything that is unnecessary overboard and pray. This reminds me of my time in the Navy. For everything, every possible eventuality, there was a set procedure, a plan, an instruction. Any deviation from the plan was against the rules. It was sin. Carried to its logical extreme in a religious environment, we call it legalism, we call it "works salvation" (which isn't of God. Grace is of God). Salvation is of God and our work to follow is obedience.

Man's idea of success is do this or else! Do that and all will be well.

The sailors are panicking, praying, and chucking things over the side, and there lay Jonah sound asleep.

One would think that someone so far out of God's will would be tormented to the point of being unable to think straight let alone sleep.

Doesn't Jonah have a conscience?

Does he FEAR God?

Some folks point to the idea of a deep sleep and say that it is the same type of sleep as Adam's when God took a rib and created Eve, but a quick check of the Hebrew Bible tells us that two completely different words are used. Adam was in a trance and Jonah is in a deep sleep.

There is the possibility that Jonah was so exhausted from running away from God that he finally collapsed, but, having been in many storms at sea, I just don't think so. Deep sleep is nigh unto impossible when the bed won't hold still and is violently moving in all directions and even comes crashing down as the next waves falls out from under the boat.

Jonah must have thought something like this, "I have given God the shake and am free. Now I can catch a nap." He had total peace. God has a great way of getting folks attention when He wants to and this storm was one monster *attention getter*.

Just a few thoughts back we saw that open doors may have nothing to do with the will of God and now we see that total peace of mind is not a strong indication of being in God's will. I don't know about you, but this challenges all that I have thought for years. Time to search the Word and pray.

The Blame Game

Jonah 1:6 So the shipmaster came to him, and said unto him, What meanest thou, O sleeper? arise, call upon thy God, if so be that God will think upon us, that we perish not.

"Get up. How can you sleep through all of this? Our gods are no help, try yours."

Did you ever notice how when things aren't going too well for some folks, they decide their god isn't working out too well for them? And then what do they do? They try to find another god or change the one they are with into something more in line with their thinking.

Designer gods. Religions pop up every day because people want a god to their own making and not one who is the creator of all things. A man created god, instead of a Creator of man. Perhaps that God is too powerful, knowing, and into everything for some folks.

We live in an age when folks have just about everything "their way." Even Frank sang that he did it "his way." One of the popular definitions of sin is "I did it my way."

Jonah 1:7 And they said everyone to his fellow, Come, and let us cast lots, that we may know for whose cause this evil is upon us. So they cast lots, and the lot fell upon Jonah.

Ah, yes, the blame game.

Remember that all of us fit into one of the following categories: we are the problem, we are part of the problem or we are part of the solution.

But, first we must acknowledge what our role in all of this is. Jonah was sleeping and the others on the ship just couldn't figure things out. They had prayed to their designer gods and nothing had changed. They had done all their procedures/works for man created salvation. Nothing changed. So, they leave it all to chance to come up with who they are to blame for this supernatural storm (predicament) they are in.

The blame game is nothing new. Matter of fact it began very early in Biblical history. Let's look at the first incident recorded. Let's go back to Genesis.

Genesis 3

1 Now the serpent was more subtil than any beast of the field which the LORD God had made. And he said unto the woman, Yea, hath God said, Ye shall not eat of every tree of the garden?

2 And the woman said unto the serpent, We may eat of the fruit of the trees of the garden

3 But of the fruit of the tree which is in the midst of the garden, God hath said, Ye shall not eat of it, neither shall ye touch it, lest ye die.

4 And the serpent said unto the woman, Ye shall not surely die:

5 For God doth know that in the day ye eat thereof, then your eyes shall be opened, and ye shall be as gods, knowing good and evil.

6 And when the woman saw that the tree was good for food, and that it was pleasant to the eyes, and a tree to be desired to make one wise, she took of the fruit thereof, and did eat, and gave also unto her husband with her; and he did eat.

7 And the eyes of them both were opened, and they knew that they were naked; and they sewed fig leaves together, and made themselves aprons.

8 And they heard the voice of the LORD God walking in the garden in the cool of the day: and Adam and his wife hid themselves from the presence of the LORD God amongst the trees of the garden.

9 And the LORD God called unto Adam, and said unto him, Where art thou?

10 And he said, I heard thy voice in the garden, and I was afraid, because I was naked; and I hid myself.

11 And he said, Who told thee that thou wast naked? Hast thou eaten of the tree, whereof I commanded thee that thou shouldest not eat?

12 And the man said, The woman whom thou gavest to be with me, she gave me of the tree, and I did eat.

13 And the LORD God said unto the woman, What is this that thou hast done? And the woman said, The serpent beguiled me, and I did eat.

JONAH

Notice how they got in trouble. They customized the words of God. They created their own personalized, designer god by making their own rules. In verses 12 and 13 we see that Adam and Eve both blamed someone else, not accepting or acknowledging any responsibility for the problem. It amazes and surprises me that Jonah will acknowledge that he is the problem.

God uses man's superstitions, even gambling (casting lots), to His purposes. Many would have us to believe that God would not use gambling or any other evil to His purpose, but we have only to look at Scripture and see the fallacy of that idea. Think of Pharoah. Look at the following Scriptures: Judges 20:9, 1 Samuel 10:20, 14:41, Nehemiah 11:1, and Acts 1:26. Romans 8:28 tells us that God uses everything to the good of them that He has called for His purposes.

A question that has come up a few times is the use of gambling proceeds by the church. A church in Florida turned down a large donation because it came from lottery winnings. In another well publicized case, a church turned down the proceeds from the sale of a liquor store. What about the harlot and the vial of ointment? Let's look at Scripture again.

Luke 7

37 And, behold, a woman in the city, which was a sinner, when she knew that Jesus sat at meat in the Pharisee's house, brought an alabaster box of ointment,

38 And stood at his feet behind him weeping, and began to wash his feet with tears, and did wipe them with the hairs of her head, and kissed his feet, and anointed them with the ointment.

39 Now when the Pharisee which had bidden him saw it, he spake within himself, saying, This man, if he were a prophet, would have known who and what manner of woman this is that toucheth him: for she is a sinner.

This woman, a sinner (a prostitute?), used ill-gotten gains to the Glory of God. Should we, as the Church, turn her down? If this is the same story as in John 12, Matthew 26, and Mark 14, the disciples tried to talk Christ into stopping her and selling the ointment to help the poor (at least Judas did). If it is not the same story, we still have the same dilemma.

Just because Satan has touched something, do we throw it out? If so, there goes printing, music, lives, and souls. Why don't we reclaim it and use it to the glory of God?

The men cast lots, drew straws, or played low man with the dice or something similar, and Jonah was the goat. He was the culprit.

What will this ship's captain and crew do with him now?

You and I both know how vicious the blame game can get.

Jonah 1:8 Then said they unto him, Tell us, we pray thee, for whose cause this evil is upon us; What is thine occupation? and whence comest thou? what is thy country? and of what people art thou?

God told the crew through the lots that Jonah knew what was going on and why.

The crew then demands that he tell them why all this is going on.

As a backslider, he is going to keep much of his relationship with God a secret. Christians do the same thing when they are not living right. He acts like a special undercover agent for the CIA instead of an overt Christian In Action.

They ask him to tell all. Achen was asked this in Joshua 7:19 just before he and his family were destroyed. Could Jonah be remembering that at this moment?

Jonah 1:9 And he said unto them, I am an Hebrew; and I fear the LORD, the God of heaven, which hath made the sea and the dry land.

Jonah is saying without thinking that God did all of this, the storm and all, because of him. God is the creator of all the land and the seas. He is the God of heaven. Jonah is one of His chosen people, a Hebrew.

Again, remember that the descendants of Abraham were supposed to bring blessings to all nations and that those who supported them were to be blessed. See Genesis 12:1-3.

He says he fears the LORD. I'll just say that his fear at this point was pretty intense. First of all he is running from the presence of God. Secondly, he is faced by a crew of mighty scared and unhappy sailors. Third, there aren't too many options open at this moment.

Note that Jonah only appears to answer two of the questions. He does not tell them he is a prophet of the most High God or that he is from the nation of Israel. He does tell them he is running from the presence of the Lord (verse 10).

At this point in time for the characters of this story, the sea equates to continued trouble, while the dry land speaks of safety for them. And God, the God that brought this storm, is responsible, in charge, and fully capable of dealing with both options.

Jonah 1:10 Then were the men exceedingly afraid, and said unto him, Why hast thou done this? For the men knew that he fled from the presence of the LORD, because he had told them.

Notice that the sailors knew what it was not to honor your god. The lost always know what a Christian should be. Look at the reaction of the "churched" folks of Jesus' day. Jesus didn't fit the mold that they had created for what a prophet and savior was going to look like and act like. So, they rejected Him, or at least most of them did.

These sailors also feared the entity that could cause and control all of nature. Wouldn't you fear something that could tear the sea apart and destroy your ship? Wouldn't you fear what could ruin all your plans and peace, your very life?

Notice that they do not recognize their own lost state. Jonah is the source of the problem. God is the cause. They just want out. The blame game is complete. They now have someone to focus every thought on rather than examine themselves.

1 Corinthians 11

31 For if we would judge ourselves, we should not be judged.

32 But when we are judged, we are chastened of the Lord, that we should not be condemned with the world.

Luke 6

37 Judge not, and ye shall not be judged: condemn not, and ye shall not be condemned: forgive, and ye shall be forgiven:

These two verses give us God's perspective on this idea.

Jonah has given them a pretty good picture of himself and his relationship with the God of this storm. Is he on the road to recovery because he is examining himself and admitting he has a problem, which he has brought them into?

Jonah 1:11 Then said they unto him, What shall we do unto thee, that the sea may be calm unto us? for the sea wrought, and was tempestuous.

The sailors are desperate; the sea is angry and tempest tossed. Their lives are on the line. They want out of this predicament alive. They just want to cruise away into the sunset with a gentle wind from abaft the beam and smooth waters. How does one appease the God of heaven and earth, land and sea, the living and the dead?

Another thought here is that every time a lost individual meets the person of God, they run into this same question, "What do I do with you that my heart will find peace?" There is no peace for the lost. There is no joy for the lost. Even in his rebellion, Jonah appears to have a lack of confusion at this point. Do we want to call that God's peace or not? Jonah is resigned to God if nothing else. The sailors don't know what to do with him, physically or spiritually.

Even so, they show more compassion than Jonah is showing toward Nineveh.

Jonah 1:12 And he said unto them, Take me up, and cast me forth into the sea; so shall the sea be calm unto you: for I know that for my sake this great tempest is upon you.

Jonah figures he deserves to die for going against God's will. We all deserve to die for going against God's will. Going against God's will is sin, and the price of sin is death.

Paul talks in Romans 5 that death came to the earth by the sin of one man and through the death of one man, Christ, life has come to man. Salvation, saved from spiritual death, comes by God's Grace through man's faith, plus or minus nothing.

Notice that Jonah shows no repentance, no sorrow, and no anguish. He has stated that it is his fault that this trouble is on them, but offers no apology or remorse. Or, is he showing his repentance and heroic sacrifice of self for others (a type of Christ, one for the many?), another of the great theological arguments. Take your pick.

He even says that this storm is on them, not us or me.

Does he even care about himself?

Okay, go back and read this verse again. Carefully. Notice that they must cast him forth into the sea. I just wonder who the first three will be that are cast into the sea. Sorry, just a bit of theological humor there.

Jonah 1:13 Nevertheless the men rowed hard to bring it to the land; but they could not: for the sea wrought, and was tempestuous against them.

No matter which way man tries or in which direction, God is against them, until they go His direction.

JONAH

In this case they are trying to save Jonah's life and keep from having to kill him themselves. Man's efforts are so puny. This is such a powerful picture of works salvation. All their efforts were to save Jonah and themselves.

Jonah does nothing, not even pray, row, or bail. Not really the kind of person you would want to die for, is he? There they are busting a gut for him, and he is doing nothing. The least he could do is jump overboard and, hopefully, save the crew. But, no, he just sits.

God's strategy works. The men on the ship cry out to Him.

Jonah 1:14 Wherefore they cried unto the LORD, and said, We beseech thee, O LORD, we beseech thee, let us not perish for this man's life, and lay not upon us innocent blood: for thou, O LORD, hast done as it pleased thee.

What tumult entered your life to cause you to cry out to Him?

Do you see the dab of faith here? They cry to the Lord whom most of them have not heard of before this day. Call upon the name of the Lord and you will be saved.

They have a real concern here because God has some strong views concerning the shedding of innocent blood.

Deuteronomy 21

8 Be merciful, O LORD, unto thy people Israel, whom thou hast redeemed, and lay not innocent blood unto thy people of Israel's charge. And the blood shall be forgiven them.

9 So shalt thou put away the guilt of innocent blood from among you, when thou shalt do that which is right in the sight of the LORD.

2 Kings 24

3 Surely at the commandment of the LORD came this upon Judah, to remove them out of his sight, for the sins of Manasseh, according to all that he did;

4 And also for the innocent blood that he shed: for he filled Jerusalem with innocent blood; which the LORD would not pardon.

Psalm 106

37 Yea, they sacrificed their sons and their daughters unto devils,

38 And shed innocent blood, even the blood of their sons and of their daughters, whom they sacrificed unto the idols of Canaan: and the land was polluted with blood.

Jeremiah 22

3 Thus saith the LORD; Execute ye judgment and righteousness, and deliver the spoiled out of the hand of the oppressor: and do no wrong, do no violence to the stranger, the fatherless, nor the widow, neither shed innocent blood in this place.

JONAH

Joel 3

19 Egypt shall be a desolation, and Edom shall be a desolate wilderness, for the violence against the children of Judah, because they have shed innocent blood in their land.

Matthew 27

3 Then Judas, which had betrayed him, when he saw that he was condemned, repented himself, and brought again the thirty pieces of silver to the chief priests and elders,

4 Saying, I have sinned in that I have betrayed the innocent blood. And they said, What is that to us? see thou to that.

All of these sailors know, to take innocent blood will harm them personally. Their own gods will never be happy with them if they cause this man to die. Their own value system leads them to try everything they know before they give up in their personal/human struggle, their works to save themselves, and toss Jonah. Obviously, they feel that if they toss Jonah, they will still die. They have no desire to die.

God grants this request of these sinners. Jonah will live. Question is, will they ever know Jonah's fate after they toss him overboard?

Jonah 1:15 So they took up Jonah, and cast him forth into the sea: and the sea ceased from her raging.

All of man's puny efforts have failed. Overboard goes Jonah.

The folks that I have seen surrender their lives to God, find that God gives an instant peace. No Jesus, no peace; know Jesus, know Peace. This peace isn't a lack of turmoil (most have much turmoil), but a total knowledge that God has a handle on things and He will only allow what is best for them.

Ah, yes. The feminine pronoun "her" for the raging sea. But, I won't get into himacanes and hurricanes at this point. It is not my desire to oppress you with too much theological humor.

Jonah 1:16 Then the men feared the LORD exceedingly, and offered a sacrifice unto the LORD, and made vows.

What a Revival! The fear of the Lord is the beginning of knowledge.

Psalm 16

11 Thou wilt shew me the path of life: in thy presence is fulness of joy; at thy right hand there are pleasures for evermore.

These men have come to know and fear the one true God. Notice that they not only fear exceedingly, they offered sacrifices and made vows.

Sounds like at this point, they began living

Romans 12

1 I beseech you therefore, brethren, by the mercies of God, that ye present your bodies a living sacrifice, holy, acceptable unto God, which is your reasonable service. And be not conformed to this world: but be ye transformed by the renewing of your mind, that ye may prove what is that good, and acceptable, and perfect, will of God.

The Fish Story

Jonah 1:17 Now the LORD had prepared a great fish to swallow up Jonah. And Jonah was in the belly of the fish three days and three nights.

In this verse we have the big picture. In the next chapter we get the details.

Great fish? In Matthew 12:40, Jesus said "ketos" which is sea monster.

In Genesis 1 and 2, during the creation, He prepared (Commissioned as a missionary) a great fish for just this purpose, and maybe others.

Wait a minute, preacher. I don't believe a great fish could swallow a man.

Good question, Johnny. Let's look at biological fact.

He created many sea monsters that will swallow a man. Sulphur Bottom Whales (Blue whales {baloenoptera musculus}) of various kinds. Whale sharks (rhinodon typicus). And others like "megamouth".

Let's look at history. Are there any incidents of a man being swallowed whole by a large sea creature? The answer is "yes."

The blue whale has a chamber in its head about 7' by 7' by 14'. Pretty large room, huh? (Bigger than some of the motel rooms I've stayed in and much larger than my bunk on the submarines I served on.) Bigger than the cells at the county jail which bunk four guys.

An article in the *Cleveland Plain Dealer* (according to Dr. J. Vernon McGee) quoted Dr. Ransome Harvey stating that a dog was found in the head of a whale six days after being lost overboard, alive and barking.

In "The Cruise of the Cathalot" by Frank Bullen, F.R.G.S., a story is told of a 15' shark being found in the stomach of a whale.

Dr. McGee also talks of James Bartley, who was thought to have been drowned after falling overboard off the Falklands, was found two days later in a whale, unconscious and alive.

Another man was billed as the "Jonah of the Twentieth Century" at the London Museum after being engulfed by a very large Whale Shark only to be found two days later unconscious and alive. After being rushed to a hospital, he was found to be suffering from shock and was released a few hours later as being physically fit. Dr. Harry Rimmer met this man in 1926 and stated that his color was odd and his body had no hair on it anywhere.

In the 12 August 2003 issue of *Weekly World News* the story is told of Rev. Paul Martinique who is reported to have been swallowed by a Humpback whale and after three days regurgitated. Rev. Martinique is reported to have said it was a test of his faith by the Lord.

JONAH

There is enough evidence of people and large animals being swallowed by various sea creatures that the possibility is not even far-fetched.

This story isn't about Jonah and the great fish. It concerns Jonah and his relationship with God. It is about God's great compassion.

And now, Jonah is separated from God.

Psalms 13

1 How long wilt thou forget me, O LORD? for ever? how long wilt thou hide thy face from me?

2 How long shall I take counsel in my soul, having sorrow in my heart daily? how long shall mine enemy be exalted over me?

3 Consider and hear me, O LORD my God: lighten mine eyes, lest I sleep the sleep of death;

4 Lest mine enemy say, I have prevailed against him; and those that trouble me rejoice when I am moved.

Do you hear the pain in this cry of David's?

How about this one?

Isaiah 59

But your iniquities have separated between you and your God, and your sins have hid his face from you, that he will not hear.

Jonah's sins have separated him from God. God hasn't moved, Jonah has.

When the time comes and you are looking for help, sometimes help comes along. When that help starts working, you don't know whether they are helping or killing you. Jonah is at the lowest point (forgive the pun) in his life. He was in trouble on the ship from the storm and the sailors. Now he is in the belly of the great fish at the bottom of the sea. So, he has been helped, but it surely doesn't appear that way to him, does it?

When you need help the most, God gets you into a position that, to you, appears totally helpless and without exit. You are in the belly of a sea monster and by all rational thinking, it is a useless, helpless, totally devastating position in which there is no sunshine, no ray of hope, no possible way of escape, not even the glimmer of a light at the end of the darkness. Isaiah 4:2 tells us that when we pass through the waters, God will be with us. Jonah doesn't have this comfort at this time.

Nahum 1

7 The Lord is good, a stronghold in the day of trouble; and He knoweth them that trust in Him.

8 But with an overrunning flood he will make an utter end of the place thereof, and darkness shall pursue his enemies.

Jonah is feeling verse 8 without much hope in verse 7. He just doesn't feel known of God, but yet he cries out to Him.

Now we get the details from inside the fish.

Jonah 2:1 Then Jonah prayed unto the LORD his God out of the fish's belly,

When did Jonah pray, right off, the whole 3 days, or after three days?

JONAH

Read verses 2 through 9 very carefully. It sounds to me like Jonah may have even been swallowed after he reached the bottom of the sea and God might have even kept him alive until the great fish swallowed him.

Jonah 2:2 And said, I cried by reason of mine affliction unto the LORD, and he heard me; out of the belly of hell cried I, and thou heardest my voice.

God doesn't hear a sinner's prayer until there is a sincere repentance in the heart or at least a sincere desire to know/draw near to God.

John 9

31 Now we know that God heareth not sinners.

Proverbs 1

22 How long, ye simple ones, will ye love simplicity? and the scorners delight in their scorning, and fools hate knowledge?

23 Turn you at my reproof: behold, I will pour out my spirit unto you, I will make known my words unto you.

24 Because I have called, and ye refused; I have stretched out my hand, and no man regarded;

25 But ye have set at nought all my counsel, and would none of my reproof.

26 I also will laugh at your calamity; I will mock when your fear cometh;

27 When your fear cometh as desolation, and your destruction cometh as a whirlwind; when distress and anguish cometh upon you.

28 Then shall they call upon me, but I will not answer; they shall seek me early, but they shall not find me:

29 For that they hated knowledge, and did not choose the fear of the LORD:

30 They would none of my counsel: they despised all my reproof.

31 Therefore shall they eat of the fruit of their own way, and be filled with their own devices.

Psalms 15

1 LORD, who shall abide in thy tabernacle? who shall dwell in thy holy hill?

2 He that walketh uprightly, and worketh righteousness, and speaketh the truth in his heart.

3 He that backbiteth not with his tongue, nor doeth evil to his neighbour, nor taketh up a reproach against his neighbour.

4 In whose eyes a vile person is contemned; but he honoureth them that fear the LORD. He that sweareth to his own hurt, and changeth not.

5 He that putteth not out his money to usury, nor taketh reward against the innocent. He that doeth these things shall never be moved.

His affliction was self-imposed by his failure to be in God's will. Our choices mean so much. Do we really understand the

JONAH

ramifications of our choices? If we do, why are we so surprised by the consequences?

In Jonah 1:2, Jonah admits he and he alone is the cause of his problem. He chose to head for Tarshish against God's will. Now, we begin to see the consequences.

Consequences are both positive and negative. We generally relate the word consequences with terrible things and not with the good. But, when we make great choices, the consequences are generally great. When we make poor choice, the adjective poor relates to the consequences.

Our God is a forgiving and patient God, but even though He forgives and forgets, we still are allowed to suffer the earthly consequences of our poor choices (sin).

Let's back up a minute and look at that idea of forgiving and forgetting.

Hebrews 10

16 This is the covenant that I will make with them after those days, saith the Lord, I will put my laws into their hearts, and in their minds will I write them;

17 And their sins and iniquities will I remember no more.

18 Now where remission of these is, there is no more offering for sin.

If He doesn't remember, He must be forgetting. Look at these;

Jeremiah 31

34 And they shall teach no more every man his neighbour, and every man his brother, saying, Know the LORD: for they shall all know me, from the least of them unto the greatest of them, saith the LORD; for I will forgive their iniquity, and I will remember their sin no more.

Isaiah 43

25 I, even I, am he that blotteth out thy transgressions for mine own sake, and will not remember thy sins.

26 Put me in remembrance: let us plead together: declare thou, that thou mayest be justified.

At this point, it seems rather evident that when God forgives, He forgets. He leaves us with the memories and earthly consequences of that sin, but that is good, because we remember the lessons learned, hopefully, and we remember that God is full of Grace to forgive us and will carry us through the consequences.

Hell, sheol or hades, a waiting place for the dead. Jonah says he is in the grave.

God doesn't hear the cries of sinful man. When His people pray He doesn't always answer the way they desire. He answers with Go, No, Whoa, or Slow.

Sometimes the answer is Go. We are given all we need then and there to meet the request. Look at Elijah and the priests of Baal in 1 Kings 18:17-40.

Sometimes the answer is No. Think of Paul and his thorn in the flesh. See 2 Corinthians 12:7-9.

JONAH

Sometimes the answer is Slow, take your time in faith and it will come. Think on the second coming of Christ as described in 1 Thessalonians 4:13-18. Sometimes this is a directional answer, which tells us to move off in this direction in faith, and God will provide along the way.

Sometimes the answer is Whoa. There just isn't an answer. That's the time to look into your relationship with God and your walk.

Jonah 2:3 For thou hadst cast me into the deep, in the midst of the seas; and the floods compassed me about: all thy billows and thy waves passed over me.

Jonah says that God threw him into the deep of the sea. So, even he doesn't hold the men on the ship responsible for his condition.

Thy waves passed over Jonah. He is completely engulfed in the waters.

Jonah 2:4 Then I said, I am cast out of thy sight; yet I will look again toward thy holy temple.

Darkness and Death. Spiritual or Physical.

Darkness points to spiritual death, separation from God. Check out the two parables in Matthew 22:13 and 25:30 (emphasis on outer darkness).

Is Jonah crying out in the last moment of his life and remembering to call on the Lord? How many people wait until they are in the deep?

Can you imagine what it would be like without the light of God in your life? The light of the world is Jesus.

John 8

12 Then spake Jesus again unto them, saying, I am the light of the world: he that followeth me shall not walk in darkness, but shall have the light of life.

John 9

5 As long as I am in the world, I am the light of the world.

Mathew 5

14 Ye are the light of the world. A city that is set on an hill cannot be hid.

Notice the shift from 'Jesus as the light of the world' to 'you are the light of the world.' With Jesus ascended to the right hand of glory, the Father's side, the believer becomes His light in this world. Think of your responsibility in this position. Don't worry. Where God commands, He gifts.

Jonah 2:5 The waters compassed me about, even to the soul: the depth closed me round about, the weeds were wrapped about my head.

He is underwater, drowned.

JONAH

Jonah 2:6 I went down to the bottoms of the mountains; the earth with her bars was about me forever: yet hast thou brought up my life from corruption, O LORD my God.

The bars point to the idea of a death cell. He has died. He has met corruption; death, sin, and even rot.

The thought here takes us into Jonah's death in the belly and then God brings him back to life. Could it be that Jonah cried out as soon as he was in the deep (verses 2-5) and then is brought back to life in the belly of the great fish to cry out some more (verses 8-9)? Both verses 6 and 7 talk of death and then life.

Now Jonah sees the truth in:

1 John 3

2 Beloved, now are we the sons of God, and it doth not yet appear what we shall be: but we know that, when he shall appear, we shall be like him; for we shall see him as he is.

3 And every man that hath this hope in him purifieth himself, even as he is pure.

We find out what we might be in Christ.

Jonah 2:7 When my soul fainted within me I remembered the LORD: and my prayer came in unto thee, into thine holy temple.

Just as he dies he remembers the Lord and the Lord hears it.

Jonah 2:8 They that observe lying vanities forsake their own mercy.

Is Jonah speaking of himself?

To "observe lying vanities" is to make empty promises to God. It is to think you can do it all on your own under your own power alone. How many think they are an island and a power unto themselves? All who deny God do. All who acknowledge God, but go their own way do just that, also.

How is it we find the ultimate power and then will not use it?

Jonah 2:9 But I will sacrifice unto thee with the voice of thanksgiving; I will pay that that I have vowed. Salvation is of the LORD.

I will pay. I will keep my word. Jonah shows his new maturity tremendously in this statement. He is now ready to do as God commands and do it with thanksgiving.

Salvation is of the Lord. The key statement of Jonah. This verse gives us the theme of this amazing book. In all of life's troubles, only the Lord has the power to save us. We may think we have a handle on things, but He's in charge.

Not only salvation, but God works with His people throughout their lives.

Hebrews 12

5 And ye have forgotten the exhortation which speaketh unto you as unto children, My son, despise not thou the chastening of the Lord, nor faint when thou art rebuked of him:

6 For whom the Lord loveth he chasteneth, and scourgeth every son whom he receiveth.

JONAH

7 If ye endure chastening, God dealeth with you as with sons; for what son is he whom the father chasteneth not?

8 But if ye be without chastisement, whereof all are partakers, then are ye bastards, and not sons.

9 Furthermore we have had fathers of our flesh which corrected us, and we gave them reverence: shall we not much rather be in subjection unto the Father of spirits, and live?

10 For they verily for a few days chastened us after their own pleasure; but he for our profit, that we might be partakers of his holiness.

11 Now no chastening for the present seemeth to be joyous, but grievous: nevertheless afterward it yieldeth the peaceable fruit of righteousness unto them which are exercised thereby.

12 Wherefore lift up the hands which hang down, and the feeble knees;

13 And make straight paths for your feet, lest that which is lame be turned out of the way; but let it rather be healed.

Jonah repented without expectation of getting out of the fish. He didn't even ask for it. But, God knows our needs.

God doesn't hesitate to receive you when you call out to Him.

John 5

24 Verily, verily, I say unto you, He that heareth my word, and believeth on him that sent me, hath everlasting life, and shall not come into condemnation; but is passed from death unto life.

25 Verily, verily, I say unto you, The hour is coming, and now is, when the dead shall hear the voice of the Son of God: and they that hear shall live.

26 For as the Father hath life in himself; so hath he given to the Son to have life in himself;

27 And hath given him authority to execute judgment also, because he is the Son of man.

Titus 3

3 For we ourselves also were sometimes foolish, disobedient, deceived, serving divers lusts and pleasures, living in malice and envy, hateful, and hating one another.

4 But after that the kindness and love of God our Saviour toward man appeared,

5 Not by works of righteousness which we have done, but according to his mercy he saved us, by the washing of regeneration, and renewing of the Holy Ghost;

6 Which he shed on us abundantly through Jesus Christ our Saviour;

7 That being justified by his grace, we should be made heirs according to the hope of eternal life.

Romans 10

13 For whosoever shall call upon the name of the Lord shall be saved.

Praise the Lord for His infinite mercy.

JONAH

Jonah 2:10 And the LORD spake unto the fish, and it vomited out Jonah upon the dry land.

Fish and sea listen to God. All of His creation listens to the Lord without reservation, except man, and the Lord works hard to bring His voice to their hearing. No other creation of the Lord's has a will except man. The Lord can make man listen, but that is in very extreme circumstances.

The miracle is here. Jonah is now back to life. Did he look partially digested as in other accounts of similar swallowings? It makes no difference, he is made whole. Just like all of us. We are dead in our sins until we cry out to the Lord and then He makes us whole.

Three days is God's timing for God's purposes, showing the death, tomb, and resurrection of Christ.

OUR GOD OF SECOND CHANCES

Jonah 3:1 And the word of the LORD came unto Jonah the second time, saying,

This is a second chance for our boy, Jonah.

How many second chances do we get?

How many second chances have you had?

Jonah gets a second chance and it is to do the same thing he was instructed to do in the first place.

Most of us will get second chances, but rarely are they the same opportunity of service or provision. Many times the second chance is a chance to do something with lesser impact, importance, or value than the first chance.

But, our God is longsuffering. He demonstrates this portion of the Fruit of the Spirit so that we can see it and use that demonstration to learn from. See also 1 Peter 3:9 and Psalm 51:12.

Remember, God never asks us to do something that He has not already done as a demonstration for us.

So, God tells Jonah,

JONAH

Jonah 3:2 Arise, go unto Nineveh, that great city, and preach unto it the preaching that I bid thee.

God gives Jonah the same command the second time, "Jonah, go give them my message," just as He did in chapter 1 verse 2.

How will Jonah handle this new old command?

How do you handle someone telling you to do the same thing you didn't want to do the first time?

Jonah is to go preaching the message he has been given. Nothing new here is there? We are to go and preach the message of the Gospel that we have been given.

How well are we responding to that task?

Remember, a request from a superior is an order, not a request. This is not God begging Jonah to do something. He is giving an order, plain and simple.

Any action other than obedience brings negative consequences. If Jonah does not go and do, he will suffer the consequences. The consequences of a second failure would probably be worse than the first. I wouldn't want to go there.

Jonah 3:3 So Jonah arose, and went unto Nineveh, according to the word of the LORD. Now Nineveh was an exceeding great city of three days' journey.

Okay, so Jonah goes where he is supposed to and is preaching as he goes. Three days journey is about 60 miles, each days travel being traditionally 20 miles.

This is a metro-plex of Khorsabad, Nineveh, and Nimrud according to most commentaries, three conjoined large cities. The wall around Nineveh was 40-50 feet high with the wall along the Tigress River 2.5 miles and the rest of the inner wall was an additional 8 miles.

Jonah 3:4 And Jonah began to enter into the city a day's journey, and he cried, and said, Yet forty days, and Nineveh shall be overthrown.

The NIV renders this as "on his first day in the city" and this seems more reasonable. Jonah begins his walk through the city, preaching as he goes. He is preaching a message he really wants to come true. He want to see Nineveh be destroyed just as they have destroyed so many of the towns of Israel.

Forty days is very significant. Let's look at the idea in depth.

Genesis 7

4 For yet seven days, and I will cause it to rain upon the earth forty days and forty nights; and every living substance that I have made will I destroy from off the face of the earth.

Noah got to see 40 days of rain after his 100 years of ship building.

Genesis 50

2 And Joseph commanded his servants the physicians to embalm his father: and the physicians embalmed Israel.

3 And forty days were fulfilled for him; for so are fulfilled the days of those which are embalmed: and the Egyptians mourned for him threescore and ten days.

Jacob took 40 days to be embalmed.

Exodus 24

18 And Moses went into the midst of the cloud, and gat him up into the mount: and Moses was in the mount forty days and forty nights.

Moses spent 40 days on the mountain getting the Law from God.

Numbers 13

25 And they returned from searching of the land after forty days.

The spies spent forty days in checking out the Promised Land.

Numbers 14

34 After the number of the days in which ye searched the land, even forty days, each day for a year, shall ye bear your iniquities, even forty years, and ye shall know my breach of promise.

Forty days of spying, one moment of doubt and 40 years in the wilderness.

1 Samuel 17

16 And the Philistine drew near morning and evening, and presented himself forty days.

Goliath taunted Israel for 40 days before David came on the scene.

1 Kings 19

8 And he arose, and did eat and drink, and went in the strength of that meat forty days and forty nights unto Horeb the mount of God.

Elijah was fortified by one meal for 40 days before he met with the enemy.

Matthew 4

2 And when he had fasted forty days and forty nights, he was afterward hungry.

Jesus fasted for 40 days before he was tempted of Satan.

Acts 1

3 To whom also he shewed himself alive after his passion by many infallible proofs, being seen of them forty days, and speaking of the things pertaining to the kingdom of God:

Jesus was with the disciples for 40 days before He ascended up to be at the right hand of Glory.

What do we see common in all of these?

Each time the 40 days was used as a preparatory time to get ready for the bigger challenge and/or miracle. Go back and read them again.

Our God is a God of second chances and He prepares His people for the work ahead.

REVIVAL

Jonah 3:5 So the people of Nineveh believed God, and proclaimed a fast, and put on sackcloth, from the greatest of them even to the least of them.

Jonah was just tickled plum pink to give Nineveh this message. He didn't want Nineveh saved. Remember back in chapter 1 we talked about our own motivation to witnessing?

Do we choose not to witness to someone out of a lack of love, a desire to not spend eternity with them, or some other idea out of our own agenda?

According to the Great Commission, we do not have a choice.

Jonah shows us a picture of obedience with an attitude, a real bad attitude.

Is your obedience to God one of *I gotta do this and that* or is your obedience one of *I wanna do His will*? Remember, Salvation = Grace + Faith + or – nothing.

Our works come out of our faith not out of fear, or a need to get shaped up first, or into salvation. Salvation cannot be earned. It is only when we quit trying to earn and surrender to His will voluntarily, without reservation that Grace appears in our lives.

The people believed God, not Jonah. When folks believe the preacher they are only beginning the journey to God. When folks come to believe God, lives change. Nothing changed in the pattern from Nineveh to this day. We are still to believe in God, not the messenger. Why is it then that so many churches falter and lose numbers when the Pastor leaves or retires? Could it be that folks were following, believing in the messenger and not the one who wrote the message?

A problem with believing the messenger and not the one who wrote the message, strange things occur like Jonestown (This was a situation where over 900 people died in a suicide/murder pact devised by their leader Jim Jones. Jones taught them that they would be translated to another planet and live happily ever after.) It is belief in the messenger that brings a 30+% loss of attendees in a congregation when a pastor leaves a church for whatever reason. It is belief in the messenger that causes many churches to split. It is belief in the messenger that allows heresies of all kinds (I just misspelled that word – kinks – somehow it fits) to be perpetrated on this world.

Think of Satan. He believed in his own message, and look where it got him and the rest of the world.

When this passage talks of the greatest down to the least, it is not an order of repentance, but a statement of inclusion. Everyone no matter what his or her status in the community must repent. You cannot be saved from the coming judgment because you paid for it, your mama was Christ's, or the membership in a congregation. All the folks of Nineveh repented from the King down to the beggar on

JONAH

the street, from the mightiest warrior to the biggest wimp. All had to come to the same heart in faith before God.

Only when a person or group of people come to repentance will we see another revival or awakening such as this one in Nineveh.

Isaac Watts said, "We see how easy it is for the Lord with one turn of His hand, with one word of His mouth, to awaken whole countries of stupid and sleeping sinners, and kindle divine life in their souls. The heavenly influence shall run from door to door, filling the hearts and lips of every inhabitant with importunate inquiries, 'What shall we do to be saved?' And, 'How shall we escape the wrath to come?'"

It won't be the Billy Grahams or the Chuck Swidolls who bring revival to our land, it will be God in the hearts of individuals.

Jonah 3:6 For word came unto the king of Nineveh, and he arose from his throne, and he laid his robe from him, and covered him with sackcloth, and sat in ashes.

The biggest part of the problem here was leadership. Where the leader goes, the group will follow.

Let me digress for just a moment. One of our problems today is not the national leadership that has forsaken God for the most part, but the home leadership which has forsaken God. When the fathers give up their responsibility to be the priests, spiritual leaders of the home, chaos will arise. Think of the Garden of Eden. Adam let Eve lead in spiritual matters without intervening and sin entered the world. When a father allows anyone else to lead in spiritual matters and he is not right there on top of it, chaos may arise. The family unit has, for the most part, been torn apart in our society and the fathers have allowed everyone but themselves to lead in the home without supervision. The family is being led by whatever is the fad of the day on the TV or in the school or even another leader in the home. When God's plan is thwarted, chaos ensues.

When folks follow God's plan, peace and life are the result.

Nineveh was following God's plan.

Jonah 3:7 And he caused it to be proclaimed and published through Nineveh by the decree of the king and his nobles, saying, Let neither man nor beast, herd nor flock, taste any thing: let them not feed, nor drink water:

8 But let man and beast be covered with sackcloth, and cry mightily unto God: yea, let them turn everyone from his evil way, and from the violence that is in their hands.

The actions the king is demanding here are totally counter to the nature of his people. They are evil and violent. The King is demanding a changed life.

Our King, Jesus, demands a changed life also. But, He provides the wherewithal to change our lives.

Jonah 3:9 Who can tell if God will turn and repent, and turn away from his fierce anger, that we perish not?

There are two kinds of sorrow shown in the Word of God and in life. The first is the sorrow of getting caught. That is what David showed when he chased down Uriah and tried to get a cover for his adulterous deed.

JONAH

The second is Godly sorrow. Godly sorrow brings a true repentance coupled with faith which leads through salvation to works which proves the truth of the faith. In other words, our faith is shown by our actions, and the action of sorrow comes from a heart ready for God's forgiveness.

2 Corinthians 7

10 For godly sorrow worketh repentance to salvation not to be repented of: but the sorrow of the world worketh death.

11 For behold this selfsame thing, that ye sorrowed after a godly sort, what carefulness it wrought in you, yea, what clearing of yourselves, yea, what indignation, yea, what fear, yea, what vehement desire, yea, what zeal, yea, what revenge! In all things

12 Wherefore, though I wrote unto you, I did it not for his cause that had done the wrong, nor for his cause that suffered wrong, but that our care for you in the sight of God might appear unto you.

When sin is the problem, repentance is the solution

The King's words are "perhaps" not "He will." No one knows the heart (plans) of God. No one knows His ways. God will do what He wills to do, in spite of man.

Romans 11

33 O the depth of the riches both of the wisdom and knowledge of God! how unsearchable are his judgments, and his ways past finding out!

Psalms 77

19 Thy way is in the sea, and thy path in the great waters, and thy footsteps are not known.

Notice, there is no presumption of mercy in these passages or in Nineveh, just committed action on the part of an entire community.

At this point, think back to the message that Jonah gave Nineveh. Was this a series of in-depth Biblical studies, a serious salvation message from a great evangelist with a smaltzy invitation dibbling with emotion at the end, or even a serious talking-to that leads to a *sinner's prayer*? The simple answer is "no." It is simply a statement of fact, God requires repentance.

Jonah 3:10 And God saw their works, that they turned from their evil way; and God repented of the evil, that he had said that he would do unto them; and he did it not.

Don't get to thinking this is a works salvation. Look at these two references.

Jeremiah 18

5 Then the word of the LORD came to me, saying,

6 O house of Israel, cannot I do with you as this potter? saith the LORD. Behold, as the clay is in the potter's hand, so are ye in mine hand, O house of Israel.

7 At what instant I shall speak concerning a nation, and concerning a kingdom, to pluck up, and to pull down, and to destroy it;

JONAH

8 If that nation, against whom I have pronounced, turn from their evil, I will repent of the evil that I thought to do unto them.

9 And at what instant I shall speak concerning a nation, and concerning a kingdom, to build and to plant it;

10 If it do evil in my sight, that it obey not my voice, then I will repent of the good, wherewith I said I would benefit them.

James 2

17 Even so faith, if it hath not works, is dead, being alone.

18 Yea, a man may say, Thou hast faith, and I have works: shew me thy faith without thy works, and I will shew thee my faith by my works.

19 Thou believest that there is one God; thou doest well: the devils also believe, and tremble.

20 But wilt thou know, O vain man, that faith without works is dead?

21 Was not Abraham our father justified by works, when he had offered Isaac his son upon the altar?

22 Seest thou how faith wrought with his works, and by works was faith made perfect?

23 And the scripture was fulfilled which saith, Abraham believed God, and it was imputed unto him for righteousness: and he was called the Friend of God.

Nineveh is showing their faith that God will *perhaps* not carry out what He has told Jonah to say to them. The warning may, in fact, carry a logical opposite in it. In other words, if they are condemned by their ways, perhaps repenting (literally a change in direction) (at this point shown by Godly sorrow and repentance) will release them from the threat of condemnation. Another true view of this is, they were agreeing with God that they deserved what God had said they would get, destruction.

The idea of God repenting, of His changing from one consequence to another is seen in this. Both options existed for Nineveh from the beginning of Jonah's calling, repent or die. Same options we have today. Nothing has changed.

It was the repentance of the people that chose the consequence. They repented so Grace applied. Had they not, wrath would have been the consequence. Nothing has changed.

In this case God responded with one of two options, where both were righteous.

He hadn't lied. He meant it when Jonah said turn or burn.

God loves to be merciful, which is one of His greatest attributes.

RESULTS AND FOLLOW UP

Jonah 4:1 But it displeased Jonah exceedingly, and he was very angry.

If the Grace of God saved your enemy, how would you feel?

Proverbs 25

21 If thine enemy be hungry, give him bread to eat; and if he be thirsty, give him water to drink:

22 For thou shalt heap coals of fire upon his head, and the LORD shall reward thee.

Romans 12

20 Therefore if thine enemy hunger, feed him; if he thirst, give him drink: for in so doing thou shalt heap coals of fire on his head.

21 Be not overcome of evil, but overcome evil with good.

God gives us some real clear statements about our treatment of enemies. It may not make much sense from a secular humanist viewpoint, but it is the way we have been treated by God Himself in sending His Son to die in our stead that we might have life and have it more abundantly.

When we see *exceedingly* or *very* in this verse, we can see that Jonah was not a happy camper. This boy was mad clear through. Jonah felt Nineveh was too bad to be worthy of God's Salvation. He, on the other hand . . .

God's behavior didn't match Jonah's desire or his inner picture of God. He didn't see the god he had created for himself, he finally saw the real God, the creator of the universe. Again we see the idea of designer gods that man creates for himself to fit his needs without having to conform to anyone else's designs on his life, might as well whittle a god out of wood or stone.

The Creator God of this world has compassion for all. Jonah couldn't or wouldn't see this. It wasn't what he wanted therefore it didn't exist in his god.

But, he prayed to this God of Creation.

Jonah 4:2 And he prayed unto the LORD, and said, I pray thee, O LORD, was not this my saying, when I was yet in my country? Therefore I fled before unto Tarshish: for I knew that thou art a gracious God, and merciful, slow to anger, and of great kindness, and repentest thee of the evil.

Jonah knew the God of Creation would do this. Jonah even gets in God's face with *"Didn't I tell you all this would happen before we started with the fish and everything?"*

He says to God, "I didn't want these people saved."

JONAH

WHY? Is hate and bitterness winning in Jonah? Does he hate Ninevites that much? Again I have to ask, why?

Perhaps this next verse tells us something of his passion against the Ninevites.

Jonah 4:3 Therefore now, O LORD, take, I beseech thee, my life from me; for it is better for me to die than to live.

In Chapter 2 he pleads to be saved, and now he begs to die. We can see his level of passion, but still no reason.

Is he saying, "I'd rather be dead than have any credit for this?"

Elijah asked the same question while hiding from Jezebel.

What they forget is that we get no credit for God working through us. It is not our work, but His. He shares the glory with us when great things happen only after we give Him the glory to begin with.

Think of David with Goliath. David says going into battle that the God of Israel will give him victory of this uncircumcised Philistine. And, He did.

Does the owner of the repaired car thank the socket?

Jonah 4:4 Then said the LORD, Doest thou well to be angry?

Joe Stowell's interpretation of this is, "Jonah, you don't want all this in the Bible, do you? I mean people are going to read it for thousands of years."

Jonah's anger is not righteous anger. For one, he does not deal with it before sundown. Secondly, it is not for others, against evil; it is against others and for evil.

Could God be asking Jonah "Is saving souls so displeasing to you?" Maybe that's something He should ask more people. I recently polled a group of Christians and found that only one out of the group of 25 or so had actually presented the Gospel to someone in the past month. "Is seeing others saved so displeasing to you?"

Notice that God does not interfere with Jonah's will. Jonah is still making his own choices. God is greatly influencing it, though, isn't He?

Mama used to say, "I can't make you obey me, but I can make you wish you had."

I'm sorry, I think a reasonable person would have caught on by now. Jonah just isn't reasonable in my mind.

Let's continue and maybe you will agree with me.

Jonah 4:5 So Jonah went out of the city, and sat on the east side of the city, and there made him a booth, and sat under it in the shadow, till he might see what would become of the city.

One commentary I read stated that the east side was uphill looking down on the city of Nineveh. Jonah wanted a great view of the city in hopes that God would not forgo the destruction of the city.

A pouting pity party time, I see.

A lousy plant Jonah will be happy about, but Nineveh? He has some real serious priority problems, or is his problem concern for himself more than for others?

Jonah 4:6 And the LORD God prepared a gourd, and made it to come up over Jonah, that it might be a shadow over his head, to

JONAH

deliver him from his grief. So Jonah was exceeding glad of the gourd.

Psalm 121

5 The LORD is thy keeper: the LORD is thy shade upon thy right hand.

6 The sun shall not smite thee by day, nor the moon by night.

God is trying to comfort and help Jonah out here and Jonah is *exceeding glad*. This boy is very happy; he is blessed because of a weed.

WOW! Jonah is just tickled plum pink over a shade weed, not to be confused with a shade tree, but yet he is mad at Nineveh and God over the saving of thousands of lives in this great city.

Jonah 4:7 But God prepared a worm when the morning rose the next day, and it smote the gourd that it withered.

First a fish, then a plant, and now a worm, God is working overtime to get Jonah's attention and Jonah just doesn't seem to appreciate it all. Perhaps he doesn't even realize he is into something big; you know, a God sized thing.

How about you?

Did He prepare you for some purpose? good works, His purpose.

Ephesians 2

10 For we are his workmanship, created in Christ Jesus unto good works, which God hath before ordained that we should walk in them.

We see through all God has prepared for Jonah's ministry that what God calls one of us to accomplish, He provides all the materials to do His will in His time.

God is done with Nineveh for a while and begins to work on Jonah. He has not only set up the task for Jonah to carry out, He has set up all that was needed to get it done. I just wonder how much of God's handiwork has gone wasted when folks have failed to respond to the call of God in their lives.

I know some of you will disagree with the idea that we are able to resist the call of God, but it surely appears Jonah did the first time. David did what he was told not to do when he numbered the people of Israel. Sin is doing what we are not supposed to do. Isn't sin thwarting the desire, the will, the call of God? Why else is it called sin, missing the mark, the whole target for our lives that God has set in place?

Conclusion time.

Jonah 4:8 And it came to pass, when the sun did arise, that God prepared a vehement east wind; and the sun beat upon the head of Jonah, that he fainted, and wished in himself to die, and said, It is better for me to die than to live.

Again, he wishes for death.

Did he keep his vow? Take another look at Jonah 2:9.

If it seems that God is not keeping His promises to you, are you keeping your promises to Him?

Jonah 4:9 And God said to Jonah, Doest thou well to be angry for the gourd? And he said, I do well to be angry, even unto death.

God asks again as He did in Jonah 4:4.

Is Jonah back talking God? Our God is big enough to take it. He is big enough to allow it within reason. How many times in the Word do we hear that somebody cried out to God? This is not always a sobbing petition. Many times this is venting the frustrations brought on by a life of faith or maybe the frustrations of not having enough faith for the moment. Think on Job. He constantly cried out in his lack of understanding. God can handle it and still love us.

People today love their pets more than other people. There is about $3,000,000,000 spent on pets annually in the USA. I wonder how that compares to the Missions budgets of the Christian churches in this country.

To God, a gourd is nothing, it has no soul, and people are everything. They are made in His image. God loves the lost. Christ came to seek and to save the Lost. God loves the Ninevites of all ages. Jonah doesn't.

He would rather die than see them saved. If it were up to him, he would buy a dog and go for a walk.

Jonah 4:10 Then said the LORD, Thou hast had pity on the gourd, for the which thou hast not laboured, neither madest it grow; which came up in a night, and perished in a night:

Jonah was exceedingly happy with the gourd. It shaded him. He claimed it as his own. Now it was dead. God's gift to him was dead and gone, wilted upon the ground. His pride and joy was dead, and he had claimed it in his heart as his own. Our pride should be in what God is doing, not what we are doing or what is happening to us; particularly, not in what we have absolutely no control over.

Again, I think back to Job. Read the last three chapters or so of Job as God asks him where he was when God built the foundations of the universe and put the stars in place, or when God gave power and strength to the horse.

He is giving Jonah the short form of that discussion here.

Jonah 4:11 And should not I spare Nineveh, that great city, wherein are more than six score thousand persons that cannot discern between their right hand and their left hand; and also much cattle?

The right hand equates to the clean hand, while the left hand is the dirty hand. For this reason many commentators feel that God is referring to children here. They would be the ones who didn't know the customs of the time and place, yet.

One of the major discussions on Jonah is God talking of 120,000 innocent children, or is He referring to the spiritually ignorant of Nineveh. Perhaps, He is referring to 120,000 fighting men as he does in many other places? In any case, there are a lot of people in Nineveh and God loves people.

End of story.

Are you disappointed?

Wouldn't you like to follow Jonah for a few more days?

JONAH

If Jonah wrote this story down we can assume one thing, but if someone else wrote it for us, there is a completely different assumption that comes to mind. We can see through this entire story that God's purposes are accomplished, sometimes in spite of His people or others. Many times they are accomplished in spite of the attitudes of many. The worst case is like Jonah when God completes His task, His desires, in spite of the Joy that is lost by the believer carrying out God's will.

Jonah missed the Joy of the Lord. I can't help but wonder, 'did he miss salvation?'

He didn't follow the number 2 law of God - Love your neighbor?

Pharisees still ask for a sign as they did in Matthew 12:38-42 when Jesus told them they already had the sign given them in this great story.

They have it. The problem of the sign is;

1 Corinthians 1

22 For the Jews require a sign, and the Greeks seek after wisdom:

23 But we preach Christ crucified, unto the Jews a stumblingblock, and unto the Greeks foolishness;

24 But unto them which are called, both Jews and Greeks, Christ the power of God, and the wisdom of God.

25 Because the foolishness of God is wiser than men; and the weakness of God is stronger than men.

How many people argue that this story cannot be true? How many get caught up in the trivia of the great fish? They have only to search as we have here to find that all the trite discussions change nothing. God did what God does. He worked supernaturally in the lives of people to show His love and concern for people, His creation.

Only an awesome God could give us real life stories such as Jonah's.

Poor Jonah. All this supernatural wonder right before him and he missed the Joy of the Lord in his own life, just like the Hebrews in the wilderness for 40 years. Man says even today that it could not be done. God did it to the amazement of even the folks that lived it.

Return and read chapter 2 again. Jonah, from what we can see here, never kept the promises he made to God. How many promises have you made to God? Did you keep them?

As a result of Jonah's (remember, the name means *dove*) ministry, the Assyrian captivity of Israel was delayed (by God of course) for about 130 years. A point Jonah will never know until judgment day.

How many times has God called you to do something that had no apparent outcome of value at the time you did it?

How many times have you asked yourself, "What has been accomplished through all my hard work and time?"

Do not miss the Joy of the Lord.

If you liked this book

try

PUZZLING THEOLOGY

also by

Pastor Doug

"PUZZLING THEOLOGY LED ME TO MY BIBLE NUMEROUS TIMES. THANK YOU FOR MAKING THAT HAPPEN."

See all his books at

www.Amazon.com/author/dougball

PS – They are not all Bible Studies.
He has westerns and stories of the not so old west, along with political suspense.

Made in the USA
Middletown, DE
01 September 2023